PROCEEDINGS

OF A

COUNCIL

OF

CONGREGATIONAL CHURCHES,

RELATIVE TO

The Church of the Puritans, New-York,

AND TO THE

PRIVILEGES OF MEMBERS THEREOF.

MAY, 1861.

NEW-YORK:

JOHN A. GRAY, PRINTER, STEREOTYPER, AND BINDER,

FIRE-PROOF BUILDINGS,

Corner of Frankfort and Jacob Streets.

1861.

PROCEEDINGS.

An *ex-parte* Council assembled at the rooms of the Geographical Society, in the city of New-York, on the 2d day of May, 1861, at 2 o'clock P.M., pursuant to the following letter missive:

Congregational Church in

Rev. and Beloved: Difficulties having arisen in the Church of the Puritans, in the city of New-York, the minority being aggrieved by the action of the majority, and feeling the need of counsel in the adjustment of said difficulties, and having requested the church to unite with them in a mutual Council, which request (a copy of which, with the main points of difficulty, is hereto annexed) has been summarily and emphatically denied, this is to invite your attendance by Pastor and Delegate at an *ex-parte* Council, to be held in this city on Thursday, the 2d day of May next, at 2 o'clock P.M., to advise us respecting the said matters of difficulty, and also with respect to the following, in addition:

As to the action of the church in summarily suspending the following-named persons, who were among the applicants for a Mutual Council, to wit: E. W. Chester, Charles Abernethy, C. R. Harvey, Geo. H. White, Thos. Rigney, and Joel Blackmer, without any form of charges or complaint being made, or any notice or intimation of trial.

It will also be respectfully submitted to the Council, whether in view of all the facts and considerations to be brought to their notice in the examination of these complaints, the interests of the Christian Church do not require that the fellowship of the churches be withdrawn from the Church of the Puritans, and it be declared no longer in connection with the Congregational body.

And it will further be submitted to said Council, whether the aggrieved members and such as may unite with them, shall not be constituted and recognized as a church of the Lord Jesus Christ, of the Congregational order, either in place of said Church of the Puritans, or otherwise, if they shall so ask of the Council.

Also all such other matter as may be legitimately connected with the foregoing main points, or with those presented to the church in connection with our request for a Mutual Council. Your brethren in Christ,

E. W. Chester,
A. S. Ball,
C. R. Harvey,
George H. White,
Seth B. Hunt,
Joel Blackmer,
Benj'n K. Phelps,

Committee of the Applicants.

Copy of the letter referred to above, presented to the Church at a regular Business Meeting, on Friday evening, March 22d, 1861:

To the Church of the Puritans, New-York City:

Whereas, Difficulties of a serious nature have for some time existed in this Church—difficulties which seem not likely to be settled by any mutual consent or agreement.

And Whereas, The undersigned and others, members of the Church, feel themselves aggrieved by the action of the majority in various matters:

And Whereas, The undersigned believe that the action of the majority in the conduct of the business of the Church, is a departure both from Congregational principles and Christian propriety:

And Whereas, Such has been the course of the Church, that in the opinion of the undersigned, there is no hope, without a change, of its being further useful, while it is so reduced in means and members, that the majority have cast it on British charity for support:

Now Therefore, In view of all these things, and of the unfortunate history of the past, looking not only to the good of this Church, but to the interests of Congregationalism and and the Christian Religion in this community, the undersigned respectfully ask the Church to agree to submit all matters in difference between them and the majority, to the advice of a Council, to be mutually agreed upon and called according to Congregational usage, hereby pledging themselves in a Christian spirit to accept and follow such advice as may by such Council be given in the premises.

And, as matters to be proposed to the said Council, the undersigned suggest and propose:

First, The course and action of the Church in regard to seeking aid from Christians in Great Britain, thus making this Church a dependent on the bounty of those who are foreigners to us.

Second, The course of the Church in the trial of Mr. Charles Abernethy, one of its members.

Third, The course of the Church in respect to its Rules and By-Laws; the undersigned claiming that these Rules and By-Laws have been repeatedly disregarded by the majority, and that in violation of them the minority have been oppressed and deprived of their just rights.

Fourth, The course and conduct of the Church in the admission of Mr. Thomas J. Hall to membership.

Fifth, The course of the Prudential Committee and of the Church, in establishing and sustaining new, and as the undersigned believe, unscriptural tests in regard to the admission of members, and the refusing admission to applicants unless they consent to pledge themselves to act with the dominant party, in party measures in the Church.

Sixth, The general course and conduct of the Church in regard to its internal affairs, and towards the Congregational body, its ministers and churches.

Seventh, Whether the best interests of the Society and Church of the Puritans, and of the cause of Christ, as represented by the Congregational body, as well as the general cause of religion in this city, do not require that the present pastoral relations existing between the Church and the Rev. George B. Cheever be dissolved.

The undersigned desire to submit these and any other matters which the Church may choose to bring forward, together with the proper specifications under the several heads, to the proposed Council for its consideration and advice. And they respectfully ask that the Church agree to such call of and submission to a Council to be mutually chosen, and that it will appoint a Committee to meet with a Committee of the undersigned, and to agree upon the ministers and churches to be called, and also to interchange with the Committee of the undersigned a statement of the matters which either party may choose to submit to the Council.

On the part of the undersigned they name as their Committee, with full powers to call a Council, and to do all acts and things in relation thereto, and also in relation to all the matters of difficulty in the Church, or growing out of or connected with the same, the following brethren, to wit:

E. W. Chester,
A. S. Ball,
C. R. Harvey,
Geo. H. White,
Seth B. Hunt,
Joel Blackmer,
Benjamin K. Phelps.

New-York, February, 1861.

(Signed)

Charles Abernethy,
Maria Abernethy,
Cornelia Abernethy,
E. F. Hull,
Geo. H. White,
Rebecca W. White,
M. A. Stevens,
S. A. Stevens,
Elisha Harris,
S. D. Bonfils,
C. B. Tompkins,
A. S. Ball,
E. W. Ball,
E. W. Chester,
C. W. Chester,
Emily E. Chester,
C. R. Harvey,
A. R. Harvey,
Olive M. Harvey,
Ellie M. Harvey,
Joel Blackmer,
E. W. Blackmer,
Seth B. Hunt,
L. De Forest Woodruff,
Wm. Henry Smith,
Samuel Ainsworth,
James J. Hull,
J. W. Halsted,
Benj. K. Phelps,
H. M. Phelps,
J. D. Platt,
W. A. Bronson,
Elizabeth Comstock,
Sarah B. Nutting,
Catherine Danforth,
Harriette Danforth,
Philena Danforth,
Sarah Gill,
E. B. Hyde,
Maria C. Hyde,
Fannie B. Hyde,
Laura L. Fitch,
Maria N. Fitch,
Harriet L. Southmayd,
Sarah A. Southmayd,
Sarah T. Field,
Joseph H. Dye,
Homer Morgan,
Elizabeth Johnstone,
Frances A. Fitch Sherwood,
A. T. Smith,
S. H. C. Smith,
Geo. F. Chester,
J. P. Chester,
Thos. Rigney,
Chloe W. Rigney,
Sarah M. Conover,
Almira J. Rigney,
Willard Harvey,
Wm. C. Gilman, Jr.,
Gerardus C. King,
Frances P. Hunt,
F. H. Hunt,
Ann Maria Judson,
Eliza Judson,
John S. Cutter,
A. Jones,
Mrs. A. Jones,
Adeline Hull,
H. A. Smith,
Sarah A. Pray,
Lucius B. Nutting,
Catherine Chamberlin,
Emma Todd,
Z. N. Bradbury,
Rachel Odell.

The Churches invited to the Council are as follows:

Congregational Church, Worcester, Mass.—Rev. Seth Sweetser, D.D.; Pastor.

The Pine Street Congregational Church, Boston.—Rev. A. L. Stone, Pastor.

Congregational Church, Andover Theological Seminary, Andover, Mass.

Congregational Church, Concord, N. H.—Rev. N. Bouton, D.D., Pastor.

Congregational Church, Pittsford, Vt.—Rev. C. Walker, D.D., Pastor.

Broadway Congregational Church, Norwich, Ct.—Rev. E. P. Gulliver, Pastor.

First Congregational Church, Hartford, Ct.—Rev. Joel Hawes, D.D., Pastor.

North Congregational Church, New-Haven, Ct.—Rev. S. W. S. Dutton, D.D., Pastor.

Second Congregational Church, Greenwich, Ct.—Rev. Joel Lindsley, D.D., Pastor.

Central Congregational Church, Providence, R. I.—Rev. L. Swain, D.D., Pastor.

Congregational Church, Albany, N. Y.—Rev. Ray Palmer, D.D., Pastor.

Congregational Church, Canandaigua, N. Y.—Rev. O. E. Daggett, D.D., Pastor.

Congregational Church, Syracuse, N. Y.—Rev. M. E. Strieby, Pastor.

Congregational Church, Newark, N. J.—Rev. W. B. Brown, Pastor.

First Congregational Church, Oberlin, Ohio.—Rev. C. G. Finney, Pastor.

Congregational Church, Jacksonville, Ill.—Rev. J. M. Sturtevant, D.D., Pastor.

Congregational Church, Chicago, Ill.—Rev. Samuel Wolcott, Pastor.

Broadway Tabernacle Church, New-York.—Rev. J. P. Thompson, D.D., Pastor.

Bethesda Congregational Church, New-York.—Rev. C. B. Ray, Pastor.

Plymouth Congregational Church, Brooklyn, N. Y.—Rev. H. W. Beecher, Pastor.

Pilgrim Congregational Church, Brooklyn, N. Y.—Rev. R. S. Storrs, D.D., Pastor.

Clinton Congregational Church, Brooklyn, N. Y.—Rev. W. J. Buddington, D.D., Pastor.

First Congregational Church, Williamsburgh, N. Y.—Rev. S. S. Jocelyn, D.D., Pastor.

South Congregational Church, Brooklyn, N. Y.—Rev. R. W. Clark, D.D., Pastor.

Bedford Congregational Church, Brooklyn, N. Y.—Rev. H. B. Elliott, Pastor.

Central Congregational Church, Brooklyn, N. Y.—Rev. J. C. French, Pastor.

New-England Congregational Church, Brooklyn, N. Y.—Rev. William R. Tompkins, Pastor.

Also Rev. Benjamin Tappan, D.D., Augusta, Me.

There were present the following members:

Park Street Church, Boston.—Rev. Andrew L. Stone, Pastor; Rev. Giles Pease, Delegate.

First Church in Concord, N. H.—Rev. N. Bouton, D.D., Pastor; Bro. Jonathan Kittredge, Delegate.

Broadway Congregational Church, Norwich, Ct.—Rev. John P. Gulliver, Pastor; Bro. Theodore McCurdy, Delegate.

North Congregational Church, New-Haven, Ct.—Rev. S. W. S. Dutton, D.D., Pastor; Dea. Nathaniel Jocelyn, Delegate.

Second Congregational Church, Greenwich, Ct.—Rev. Joel H. Lindsley, D.D., Pastor; Rev. Mark Mead, Delegate.

Congregational Church, Albany, N. Y.—Rev. Ray Palmer, D.D., Pastor; Dea. A. S. Kibbe, Delegate.

Congregational Church, Canandaigua, N. Y.—Dea. Henry W. Taylor, Delegate.

Plymouth Church, Syracuse, N. Y.—Rev. M. E. Strieby, Pastor; Bro. Ira H. Cobb, Delegate.

Congregational Church, Newark, N. J.—Rev. W. B. Brown, Pastor; Rev. George Brown, Delegate.

Congregational Church, Jacksonville, Ill.—Rev. J. M. Sturtevant, D.D., Delegate.

New England Church, Chicago, Ill.—Rev. Samuel Wolcott, Pastor.

Broadway Tabernacle Church, New-York City.—Rev. Joseph P. Thompson, D.D., Pastor; Dea. Austin Abbott, Delegate.

Clinton Avenue Church, Brooklyn.—Rev. Wm. J. Buddington, D.D., Pastor; Dea. Earl E. Miles, Delegate.

Congregational Church, South-Brooklyn.—Rev. Rufus W. Clark, D.D., Pastor; Bro. Wm. P. Libbey, Delegate.

Bedford Congregational Church, Brooklyn.—Rev. Henry B. Elliott, Pastor; Rev. W. J. Relyea, Delegate.

First Congregational Church, Paterson, N. J.—Rev. C. H. A. Bulkley, Pastor.

Central Congregational Church, Brooklyn.—Rev. J. C. French.

Rev. Dr. Sturtevant was chosen Moderator, Rev. Dr. Dutton, Scribe, and Rev. Mr. Elliott, Assistant-Scribe.

The Council united in prayer with the Moderator. The First Congregational Church in Williamsburgh, in a letter which was read, declined acting with the Council. Letters were read from Rev. Dr. Hawes, of Hartford, and Rev. Dr. Walker, of Pittsford, Vt., expressing their desire to be present with Council, regretting that circumstances made it impossible. A communication from those calling the Council, expressing their motives, and stating that they had requested Rev. Dr. Bacon to act as their advocate, was read by one of their Committee, E. W. Chester, Esq.

The following resolutions were unanimously adopted:

Resolved, That a Committee of three be appointed to notify the Church of the Puritans that this Council is in session, and to invite them to accept this as a mutual Council for the settlement of difficulties pending between themselves and the parties calling this Council. Should this invitation be declined, that they be invited to present to the Council such information as the Council may deem relevant.

Resolved, That the Committee be instructed to request from that Church, in any event, the use of their records for the guidance of the Council.

Rev. Dr. Clark, Judge Taylor, and Rev. Mr. Strieby were, by nomination, appointed such Committee.

On motion of Dr. Bouton the Council proceeded to the hearing of the case.

Dr. Bacon's Remarks.—Dr. Bacon said he had taken no part in preparing the case as it is now to be submitted to this Council. He had had no consultation with the parties making their appeal to this Council for advice, prior to their applying to the Church for a mutual council. Their application for a mutual council is presented in the letter of missive, and also the additional matter which the subsequent action of the Church on the application of the complainants for a mutual council made necessary. He had only proposed himself to give the complainants such advice and assistance as he might be able to give, in laying before the Council what he conceived to be those principles of ecclesiastical order and of Christian discipline, and of the fellowship of the churches which were involved in this case, and which are important, not only to the applicants for this Council, but important to this Church, and important to the whole community of Congregational churches, and to the Church of Christ at large. If these complainants had expected such important events as had taken place within the past few days in our national affairs, they would not have issued their letter calling this Council. Yet in some respects the time had its advantages for the hearing of this case. One important consideration was, that the newspapers had plenty to occupy them without attempting to report the doings of this Council. It had been one of the chronic misfortunes of the Church of the Puritans, always to be in the newspapers. In other times, too, the difficulties in this church had always been aggravated by the supposed relation that they had to great political questions. Certainly nobody will say now that this Council has come together to put down anti-slavery in the Church of the Puritans. He might add, that in the selection of this Council it was intended that a large proportion of churches recognized as unequivocally opposed to slavery should be represented. The list of the churches sent to is sufficient evidence on that point.

Dr. Bacon here read the Charges:

First. The course and action of the Church in seeking aid from Christians in Great Britain, thus making this Church a dependent on the bounty of those who are foreigners to us.

ITEMS.

First. This mission was *secretly* planned and commenced by the pastor and four other members of the Church.

Second. This movement was necessarily schismatic, and could not result otherwise than in a division of the Church, unless it or the Congregational characteristics of the Church should be abandoned.

Third. The *plan* of the authors of this mission contemplated and anticipated the necessity of continuing Dr. Cheever in the Church of the Puritans in *spite* of the Church and congregation, or, as an alternative, taking him from the church to lead another enterprise. In either event they expected a division of the Church.

Fourth. The inauguration of this mission was not honest towards the Church, for, while their agent was at work in Great Britain, she was enjoined from giving publicity to her operations by her employers on this side. Notwithstanding this injunction, a report that the Church of the Puritans was begging for money in a foreign land found its way hither. This report was immediately contradicted by an editorial in *The Independent*, the pastor of the Church being at the time one of its regular contributors. Yet the contradiction was suffered to be accepted by his people as presenting the truth in the premises, and *here the Church rested until the appearance of the "Spurgeon letter."* Again, the mission having been brought to light by the publication of this letter in New-York, the authors of the appeal sought to shirk, in a measure, the responsibility of their conduct, by representing in substance that inasmuch as Miss Johnstone was about to make a visit to her friends in Great Britain, a favorable opportunity presented to seek a little pecuniary aid from British philanthropists to save "the citadel of anti-slavery" on Union Square from being surrendered to the enemy. Whereas, when the truth became known, it was ascertained that the only object Miss Johnstone had in going to England was to obtain funds for the Church of the Puritans.

Fifth. At a meeting of the Church, held in the month of November, 1859, a portion of the Church voted in favor of "exonerating from all blame in the premises" those who had commemced the mission. Since that time, fidelity to the "British aid" appeal has been the principal test of fellowship with a majority of the Church.

Sixth. Any funds obtained as the fruit of this mission, although sought for in the name of the Church, do not come under the control of the Church or Society, but are held by the pastor and such others as *he chooses* to associate with him; nor do they pass from their hands except at their option. Thus an irresponsible money power is created, making the pastor independent of his people for that support which constitutes an important bond of union between him and his flock.

Second. The course of the Church in the trial of Mr. Charles Abernethy.

ITEMS.

First. In entertaining charges which were frivolous in their nature.

Second. In entertaining said charges, not with a view to Christian discipline, according to the letter and spirit of the Gospel, but for partisan purposes and in the spirit of persecution.

Third. In refusing the accused an open and speedy trial, notwithstanding his earnest and expressed desire for such trial.

Fourth. In postponing the trial by an unreasonable adjournment.

Fifth. In taking no notice of the case at the time to which the meeting was adjourned.

Third. The course of the Church in respect to its Rules and By-Laws; the undersigned claiming that these Rules and By-Laws have been repeatedly disregarded by the majority, and that in the violation of them, the minority have been oppressed and deprived of their just rights.

ITEMS.

First. In overriding the Prudential Committee, as in the case of Mr. Thomas J. Hall. See Third and Eighth Standing Rules.

Second. In repeatedly preventing members from speaking to motions, according to the "Regulations for Business Meetings."

Third. In the refusal by the Clerk to notify Business Meetings, as provided for in the Sixth Standing Rule.

Fourth. In the refusal of the Church to unite at the request of members, in calling a mutual council for the settlement of difficulties. See Second Standing Rule.

Fifth. In its disregard of the Tenth Standing Rule in its treatment of members whom it would subject to Church censure.

Fourth. The course and conduct of the Church in the admission of Mr. Thomas J. Hall to membership.

ITEMS.

First. In violently setting aside the action of the Prudential Committee, while they had the application of Mr. Hall under advisement, and were proceeding with all due diligence.

Second. In refusing to allow a reasonable time and opportunity for the settlement of a serious difficulty which was known to exist between Mr. Hall and members of the Church, and which had arisen subsequently to his having obtained his letter of dismission from the Church with which he had been connected.

Third. In refusing those who had objections to his admission, the opportunity of stating those objections at the time the vote to admit him was declared to have been passed.

Fifth. The course of the Prudential Committee and of the Church, in establishing and sustaining new, and as the undersigned believe, unscriptural tests in regard to the admission of members, and the refusing admission to applicants unless they consent to pledge themselves to act with the dominant party, in party measures in the Church.

ITEMS.

First. A lady, the wife of one of the members of the Church, bringing a letter from a sister Church, regular in its form in every respect, was rejected by the Prudential Committee because she declined to answer affirmatively the following questions: First. Whether she was in favor of the British Aid Mission? and Second. Whether she would vote to continue Dr. Cheever as pastor?

Second. It has become the settled policy of the majority to discourage accessions to the Church, upon the simple acceptance of the articles of faith and the covenant, as in former times, by oft-repeated declarations, that none would be received except such as would agree beforehand to sustain the British Mission, and Dr. Cheever as the pastor.

Sixth. The general course and conduct of the Church in regard to its internal affairs, and towards the Congregational body, its ministers and churches.

ITEMS.

First. The systematic and persistent misrepresentation of the complainants, particularly of certain individuals among them. These misrepresentations relate both to facts and motives, and are embodied in reports of Church Committees, and in speeches made by members of the majority, and when the attention of the Church has been directed to them, the injured parties have not only been denied a hearing, but have been further charged with being schismatics and covenant-breakers.

See the report made by a committee consisting of Rev. George B. Cheever, Rev. C. J. Warren, and Dexter Fairbank, in reply to the protest of twenty-two members, against the admission of Mr. Thomas J. Hall. Also the report of a committee consisting of Messrs. Dexter Fairbank, H. A. Hartt, Edwin West, Edward Gilbert, William E. Whiting, ——— Semple, Kenyon Cox, and Rev. S. R. Davis, adopted by the Church on the evening of March 22, 1861.

Second. The persistent and oft-repeated declaration in substance, by the pastor, as agent of the Church, and by Committees in their published statements, that the signers of the "Protest to the Christian Public of Great Britain," were a pro-slavery faction, and that they opposed Dr. Cheever *because* of his fidelity to the great cause of anti-slavery, whereas it is notorious that these same persons had sustained and kept the pastor in his place, *because* of his anti-slavery principles.

Third. The administration of the affairs of the Church with the single purpose of sustaining Dr. Cheever, *through* the agency of the British Mission, and this while the Church are kept in profound ignorance of its condition and prospects.

Fourth. The virtual withdrawal of the Church from the sympathies and fellowship of the Congregational churches, by its refusal, at the request of aggrieved parties, to unite in calling a mutual council.

Fifth. The necessary result of the teachings of the majority, in their exhortations at conference meetings, and in the reports of their committees respecting the fellowship of the churches of the Congregational order, is, that it is not worth retaining, inasmuch as they are uniformly pro-slavery, and their pastors are all dumb dogs, and bitterly opposed to Dr. Cheever and the Church of the Puritans.

Seventh. "Whether the best interests of the Society and Church of the Puritans, and the cause of Christ as represented by the Congregational body, as well as the general cause of religion in this city, do not require that the present pastoral relations existing between the Church and Rev. George B. Cheever be dissolved."

ITEMS.

First. The Church as it existed a few years since, was numerous, influential for good, and strong in unity. It is now feeble in numbers, helpless in resources, and powerless for good.

Second. The history of the past four years demonstrates that the present pastor can not be expected to be instrumental in reëstablishing the Church on the foundations of Gospel truth and practice.

Third. Because, in our belief, he makes himself the minister of a party and not of the Church.

Fourth. Because, a difference of opinion honestly held, respecting questions of policy in the Church, seems to be a sufficient cause for treating those who thus differ from him, as personal enemies, and enemies of the cause of righteousness, thus alienating them from the Church, until they feel compelled to retire to other churches.

Eighth. As to the action of the Church in summarily suspending the following-named persons, who were among the applicants for a mutual council; to wit: E. W. Chester, Charles Abernethy, C. R. Harvey, George H. White, Thomas Rigney, and Joel Blackmer, without any form of charges or complaint being made, or any notice or intimation of trial.

Ninth. It will also be respectfully submitted to the Council, whether in view of all the facts and considerations to be brought to their notice in the examination of these complaints, the interests of the Christian Church do not require that the fellowship of the churches be withdrawn from the Church of the Puritans, and it be declared no longer in connection with the Congregational body.

Tenth. And it will be further submitted to said Council, whether the aggrieved members and such as may unite with them, shall not be constituted and recognized as a Church of the LORD JESUS CHRIST, of the Congregational order, either in place of said Church of the Puritans, or otherwise, if they shall so ask of the Council.

These complainants, continued Dr. BACON, are altogether another party from that which called a previous *ex parte* Council on the difficulties in this Church. The persons calling this Council were among the most earnest and devoted friends of the pastor at that time, and the difficulties which come before this Council, have no sort of connection with the difficulties that came before that former Council, unless it is said that the pastor of the Church is that connection. These difficulties began where the statement that had just been read begins, with the sending of an agent to Great Britain on a begging expedition to raise funds for the Church of the Puritans on Union Square.

The Committee appointed to confer with the Church of the Puritans reported that they had ascertained that there would be no meeting of the Church of the Puritans until Friday evening. They then sought the clerk of the Church, but were unable to find him, and were informed that he is probably out of the city. They then requested Dr. West, a member of the Prudential Committee of that Church, to inform the officers of the Church of the action of the Council, and he promised to do so.

Rev. Dr. BOUTON said he understood that the Pastor of the Church of the Puritans was absent, and the trouble in his mind was, as to the propriety of action in any regard whatever, that would affect the pastor, while he is absent and unable to defend himself.

Dr. BACON said, that the absence of the pastor of the Church was not accidental. He had been absent nine months, and his return was as uncertain as the return of some unknown comet. It had been proposed by the complainants that the question of the continuance of the relation of Dr. Cheever with the Church should be committed to a mutual Council; but as the Church refused to unite in calling such a Council, he supposed this Council would not act on that matter.

Dr. Ball, one of the complainants, said they had endeavored for months to arrive at some information in relation to Dr. Cheever's return, and those who have corresponded with him had failed to communicate to the Church, any statement in reference to any definite time. By the vote of the Church, he went to England a few months for his health; and no vote was taken to make him an agent for the collection of money.

Dr. Bacon said there was no intention or desire on the part of the complainants, to invite this Council to pass any judgment whatever upon the character or standing of Dr. Cheever.

After a considerable discussion, a resolution was adopted, requesting the complainants to avoid such testimony as merely pertained to the character or action of Dr. Cheever, as he was not present to defend himself.

The Council then took a recess until evening.

EVENING SESSION.

THE BRITISH AID MISSION.

Dr. Bacon proceeded to read testimony in proof of the first complaint.

The letter of Dr. Cheever to Mr. Spurgeon in reference to the British Aid Mission.

No. 21 East Fifteenth Street, New-York,
September 1st, 1859.

My Dear Sir: On my return to the city, I find letters from England, making inquiries with regard to Miss Johnstone, a member of my Church, now endeavoring to procure some aid for us in the conflict in which we are engaged against slavery and the slave power in this country. A number of individuals have been suggested as important to be addressed and put in possession of the facts in regard to the appeal; but, as I am compelled immediately to leave the city again for a little season, and am overwhelmed with engagements, it is quite impossible to meet these suggestions. I have therefore taken the liberty of sending you a copy in part of a letter written to a person in England, in reply to inquiries on this subject. I do this in order that, whether any material aid through Miss Johnstone's effort on our behalf should have been gained or not, it may be seen and known that her appeal is authentic, and that some of the grounds may be made manifest, on which such an effort has become necessary. In answer to an individual making inquiries from England, I have written as follows: "Your inquiries as to Miss Johnstone's effort and the necessity of it, are natural and just. We did not anticipate nor intend the publicity given to her mission, if it can be so called, but supposed she would, in a quiet and private way, present our cause, she herself possessing the greatest possible confidence of success. From the very urgency of the case and the greatness of our danger, being not only surrounded by enemies without, but beset by foes within, we could not ourselves take any church action concerning this appeal; but a few of us, convinced that we must have aid from some quarter, or be conquered, consented that Miss Johnstone should make what effort she could in Great Britain, and gave her our authentication. At the same time, we made every effort for aid from friends here outside our own Church, and, by God's blessing, met with such success that we were carried safely through the financial year, and entered on the necessary arrangements for another. By the entire dismissal of the disaffected party in our Church, we are now stronger in the spirit and strength of harmony and unity, but much weakened in pecuniary ability, so that the same appeal for aid must be renewed, and efficient aid must be given, in order that we may be enabled to maintain this citadel of Christ's free Gospel amidst such continued and strenuous efforts for our defeat. I assure you that we do greatly need whatever aid we can get. If it please God to keep us, we shall be kept, and he will provide the way, whether through friends here or abroad. But the conflict is terrible, and the pressure of prejudice, fashion, wealth, power, anger, wrath, and malice against us, with the weight of all the Christian conservatism of the country denouncing our course, and slandering us as Robespierres and fanatics, render it next to impossible for us to increase in numbers or ability, for men will not join us, except it be here and there a true-hearted abolitionist whom God sends.

God has stirred up some such, and brought them from other churches to ours, and this one thing has been our preservation, for without such aid we must have gone down. But at present no new friends come to our support, while yet the battle waxes hotter and more desperate; and, what is exceedingly depressing and discouraging, the moment we begin to be in arrears financially, the timid and half-hearted ones among us, perhaps fearful lest the whole burden may fall upon them, begin to declare that we must give up all idea of sustaining ourselves; that it is useless to attempt doing this any longer; that it is manifest that preaching against the sin of slavery is so horribly unpopular that if any man or church undertake it they can not be supported, but must fail; that we had better give up when we can do so with some dignity, and not be starved out. This cowardice, and the croakings that grow out of it, are most injurious to our cause. We can depend only on a very few. Meantime, *there is greater need than ever of just such sermons against slavery as I have been preaching*, only a thousand times more able and energetic; and to give up my pulpit now, would be disastrous in the extreme to the cause of Christian abolitionism. It would put an end to any freedom of the pulpit and of God's word against this gigantic sin; but our expenses are so heavy, in consequence of fifteen hundred dollars ground rent, in addition to all the ordinary charges of a prominent church in the city, that we can not ourselves meet them; and my course in proclaiming God's word so freely and fully against slavery and slaveholding as the sin of man-stealing, set by God in the same catalogue with murder, is so unpopular, arrays all the Christian expediency of all the churches against us with so much bitterness, that it would be quite impossible to make any appeal for aid with any hope of success, even to the churches of our own denomination. Too many of them heartily desire our downfall, and, I suppose, expect year after year to see it. That we have been sustained as we have is a wonder, *and to maintain the miracle*, if it may please God to maintain it, *we must still have pecuniary aid.* My Church will keep united, and will rally round me in defense of my preaching against slavery, only while the few who do not intend to relinquish the struggle are enabled to provide the ways and means of meeting our deficiencies. While we can do that, we can, with a tolerable degree of confidence, rely on a good majority in our favor, and can keep the Church; but the moment we are swamped in money matters, that moment we are overthrown. While God gives me grace, health, and strength, and continues the opportunity, I mean to reïterate my efforts with the sword of the Spirit, which is the word of God. I am endeavoring to reach the conscience of the churches and the ministry in regard to this sin, and to rouse up both to united action against it. If it please God that his word shall once be freely and generally proclaimed against it, it can not stand. If he add his Spirit, and really set his Church on fire against the iniquity of making merchandise of men, then we shall see a greater moral and spiritual triumph than the world has ever witnessed since the first age of the Gospel. The manifest abolition of this gigantic and infernal wickedness by the word and Spirit of God, even after it had been enthroned as the supreme law and policy of our nation, the dictate of our justice, the fruit of our religion, would be so glorious a conquest, so full of praise to God, and of shame to wicked men, and unbelievers, and scoffers, that it is to be infinitely desired and ceaselessly labored after. And, though sometimes we are almost in despair, yet, when we remember that the word of God has really not yet been tried in the conflict, but excluded from it, muzzled, suffocated, buried in silence, or perverted into the sanction of the sin, so that its omnipotence is a power yet in reserve, we can not but hope that God intends this mighty and glorious demonstration, and that, when we are driven more despairingly to him, and it is perfectly manifest that neither politics, nor statistics, nor theories of free soil, nor free labor, even the profit of freedom, nor any political party, nor any demonstrations of science or philanthropy, can save us, then he will set some souls on fire, and let loose the thunderings and lightnings of his word, as in the first great Reformation, with such overwhelming majesty that nothing can stand against it. I am a very poor hand to make a beginning—a poor, miserable vessel for such fire—and yet I am constrained into it, and can not draw back; and as there must be a beginning in some quarter, or no conflagration or cannonading at all, it may as well begin in our Church and my ministry as any where else, if God pleases. And it is a solemn fact that almost no where else is the word of God proclaimed freely, fully, persistently, on the Sabbath, against this sin. A paragraph is sometimes let off, or a sermon on a fast-day; and if this is not followed by disturbance and wrath henceforward, on the score of that solitary demonstration, the minister and Church profess to be sufficiently anti-slavery, and unite in opposing any church or minister that will go much further; there is no purpose whatever for the abolition of the sin. Indeed, the very men who boast of being anti-slavery are opposed to abolitionism, and denounce the abolitionists. So that really, in some respects, things are in about as bad a state as they can be, and in many quarters the most diabolical pro-slavery spirit is conjoined with the highest profession of piety and orthodoxy. It is a perfectly wonderful thing, that *a real*, *thorough*, *abolition orthodox Church*, *such as mine to a good degree is*, can have been trained and supported so long in the heart of a city such as New-York, so large a portion both of the ecclesiastical and mercantile community being in league with slaveholders for the protection of their sin. Meantime, we get no aid from visitors who come to us from abroad, from your country or elsewhere, for they are always persuaded into a most politic silence, and, having generally some object to accomplish, they desire to keep on the best terms with all parties, and on the whole, generally are persuaded into the impression that the Abolitionists are a very injudicious and fanatical set of men, and that the sin of slavery has more to be said in apology on its behalf than Abolitionists are willing to admit. They can not think that so many good men as they meet with in connection with this sin are wholly mistaken or wholly guilty in sanctioning it for a time in some degree. Thus their influence is with the slave power, not against it, and they themselves, especially after traveling South, lose their horror of the cruelty and the crime, and begin to think that there is no cruelty and little guilt inhering in it, but that the great guilt lies in the course of these radical men, who do not cease, on the authority of God, to proclaim slavery and slaveholding as sin, and only sin, continually. I wish, with all my heart, that I could come to England, but it is not possible just now. I can not leave my post, if God gives me the strength and the possibility to continue it. The people of England have very little idea of the terrible extent to which the sanction of slavery, and opposition against all agitation about it as a sin, have got possession of the churches, so that the revivals of religion and the revival of the slave-trade may go together without any quarrel. Or, if there be any outcry against the foreign slave-trade, there is an equally earnest outcry, and much more bitter, against all those who denounced the domestic slave-trade and American slavery. Of a truth, we are in a dreadful state, and I do not see any way of avoiding the wrath of God, or any escape from ruin except by his word and Spirit—his word proclaimed against the reigning guilt, and his Spirit in accompanying the proclamation. Pardon this long letter: be assured *whatever aid you may be able to gain for us, or whatever help you can extend to Miss Johnstone in getting aid, is truly and greatly needed, and will be most thankfully received.*

I am glad to hear that Frederick Douglas is to be in England this winter. He is a remarkable man. I had the pleasure of listening to an address from him on the recent anniversary of West-India emancipation—a most eloquent and powerful speech, that would have done credit to Mr. Webster, had he been capable of its moral elevation.

I am about publishing a new work on the guilt of slavery and the crime of slaveholding demonstrated by the Old and New Testament Scripture; and such is the unpopularity of the subject that my publishers will not issue it, and I am obliged to publish it by subscription on my own responsibility. With the highest respect, yours most truly, George B. Cheever.

Rev. C. H. Spurgeon.

The resolution of the Board of Trustees disavowing all connection with Miss Johnstone's mission:

At a meeting of the Board of Trustees of the Church of the Puritans, held Monday evening, November 14th, 1849, the following preamble and resolutions were unanimously adopted:

Whereas, This Board learn through the public prints that a Miss Johnstone has made appeals to the people of Great Britain for funds to sustain the Church of the Puritans, and it appears by a letter from the pastor, addressed to the Rev. C. H. Spurgeon, of England, that he (the pastor) and some individuals have authorized Miss Johnstone to collect money in Great Britain for this purpose; and

Whereas, In the opinion of this Board, such an appeal is contrary to the best interests of the Church and Society, and calculated to injure them in the estimation of the Christian public, since the contributions sought are for the purpose of meeting the ordinary expenses of worship, which rightfully belong to the congregation to pay:

Resolved, therefore, That this Board disavow all responsibility for the acts of Miss Johnstone, as unauthorized by the Society or its Trustees.

Statement of the reasons for the British Mission, made by Dr. H. A. Hartt for the authors of the appeal:

The following statement of reasons for Dr. Cheever's appeal to the abolitionists of Great Britain on behalf of the Church of the Puritans, was read at the meeting of the Society on Tuesday evening:

The publication of a letter from the Rev. Dr. Cheever to the Rev. Mr. Spurgeon, with reference to an appeal to the churches in Great Britain for sympathy and aid in his conflict with the slave power, has produced considerable excitement and remark. A portion both of the religious and secular press have thought it necessary to comment upon it with great earnestness, and to make it the occasion of severe and bitter strictures upon the ministerial character and labors of Dr. Cheever.

The Trustees of the *Society* of the Church of the Puritans have also felt themselves called upon to publish a series of resolutions, disavowing all responsibility for the measure, and expressing their disapprobation of it—thus placing themselves before the world in direct antagonism with the pastor.

Under these circumstances, the authors of the appeal deem it their duty to state freely and fully the reasons which led them to make it, and which, in their opinion, rendered it necessary and right. An article has already appeared on the subject, by one of our number, which, though unanswerable in its argument, was open to the charge of personality and vituperation. The writer is a young man who has only recently been converted under the ministry of Dr. Cheever. Like Peter, in his indignation, he seized a sword and cut off the ear of a servant of the High Priest, and, as the age of miracles is past, it can not be healed; but he has already repented, and now again appears in the field, with tempered zeal and chastened spirit, to do good service, we trust, in the cause of truth, and to strengthen his brethren.

The removal of the disaffected parties from the Church, after a protracted and bitter controversy, inspired Dr. Cheever and his friends with the hope of permanent peace, and a full triumph of those great principles for which they had contended. But it soon appeared that the opposition remained.

At a meeting of the Trustees in December last, the Treasurer reported a debt of $3500, whereupon one of those gentlemen said that he would not give a dollar towards the payment of it, and advised, as the only means of saving the Church, that Dr. Cheever should be dismissed, and the band of his enemies who had left should be recalled. Another said he had only remained in the Church for a long time because it was in trouble, *but he would give nothing.* One gentleman also was present, and took part on that occasion, who had withdrawn his membership in consequence of his dissatisfaction with the pastor's ministry. These facts were mentioned by an officer of the Board of Trustees to one of the authors of the appeal, and he assured him, at the same time, that the Church must go down, and further remarked that, in his opinion, no thorough anti-slavery ministry could be sustained in the city of New York.

Immediately after this meeting, a statement appeared in a letter of the New-York correspondent of a Boston journal, that Dr. Cheever had resigned.

It was obvious that dissatisfaction existed, and there was reason to fear that at the annual meeting in March, when the debt should be announced, it would be seized and set forth as an evidence of the inefficiency and unpopularity of the pastor's ministry, and a proposition be made for his removal.

In order to obviate this danger, Dr. Cheever and one of his warmest supporters made a special effort, and succeeded in obtaining from parties in and out of the Church about one half the amount of the debt.

At the annnal meeting, when the announcement was made that this sum had been raised and deposited in the bank, the opponents of Dr. Cheever saw that their plan was defeated. An official member of the Church then offered to give $250 towards the remainder of the debt, provided the whole amount should be raised by the 1st of May, and $1000 pledged to meet the probable deficiency of the next year. Others followed with promises of various sums upon a similar condition. It was thought by some that the demand for the pledge was unnecessary; but, in order to secure the amounts thus proposed, it was given on the spot — the young men of the Church, with a noble generosity, offering from $25 to $100 each from their limited incomes.

The hope was cherished that, after this demonstration, the disaffected parties, seeing that their designs were frustrated, would give up their opposition.

After the annual meeting about $800 of the debt still remained, and a Committee was appointed to raise this amount by the 1st of May.

Meanwhile an application was made to the Church by the agent of the Congregational Union for a contribution to aid weak churches in the West; $3000 were subscribed. A large portion of the sum was given by those who can not be relied upon in an extremity brought on by a conflict with the slave power, and several wealthy members who would not give one dollar toward the liquidation of the debt contributed $250 each for this object.

In the end, a few who are devoted to the principles of freedom were obliged, in order to secure the sums conditionally pledged, to postpone for a time the payment of the money they had promised to the weak churches in the West, and apply them to their own weak Church in the East.

On the 1st of May the debt was paid, but our wealthy friends, instead of returning to their duty, resigned their pews, and $1000 of our ordinary revenue were struck off.

In the midst of these perplexities a few of us who believed that we enjoyed the confidence of the majority of the Church, with the concurrence of Dr. Cheever, deemed it advisable to appeal to our brethren in England. We knew that if we laid the matter before the whole body, or even advised with a large number of those who sympathized with us, it would receive immediate publicity, bring down upon our heads a storm such as is now pelting us from every quarter, and, what was of infinitely more consequence to us, set our enemies on the alert, and give them an opportunity of throwing obstacles in our way, from the start, on the ground where we designed to work. We addressed a letter to the British churches, in which we simply gave an outline of the conflict in which the Church of the Puritans had been engaged for a few years past with the slave power, and its consequent losses and embarrassments, carefully abstaining from all allusion to internal dissensions, dissatisfaction, or apprehended treachery. We committed it to the charge of Miss Johnstone, a member of the Church, who was desirous of visiting her friends in Scotland, with instructions that she should present it to the clergymen of different denominations who sympathized with us on the question of slavery, in order to raise funds, not only sufficient to secure us against the possibility of a present defeat, but also, if possible, to establish a foundation of $20,000 or $30,000 for the perpetual liquidation of the ground-rent.

Through some mistake it fell into the hands of a correspondent of the *National Anti-Slavery Standard*, and was noticed as an item of news in a communication to that paper. Immediately the *Independent*, without inquiry of Dr. Cheever, published an editorial on the subject, treating it as a hoax, and representing the Church of the Puritans as in a most flourishing condition. The reasons which induced us to avoid publicity at first, prevented us from answering that editorial, but inasmuch as it placed Miss Johnstone in a false position in Great Britain, and threw a serious difficulty in the way of her mission, we were of course obliged to meet it there. Dr. Cheever was directly applied to by a person in England, and the substance of his reply, afterwards sent to Mr. Spurgeon, is the document which is now producing so much disturbance.

We are happy to say that we have just received the most cheering intelligence from Great Britain that our faith in the sympathy of Christians there was well founded, and that there is every probability that the mission will succeed. The head and heart of all Christendom outside this country—ay, and *in* this country, too, far more than men dream of—respond to the sentiment uttered by the Archbishop of Canterbury to Hon. Charles Sumner, "that Christianity and slavery ought not to be mentioned in the same day."

But why may not the faithful friends of freedom, persecuted and sorely pressed by the slave power, go for aid and comfort where that sentiment is not only cherished as a thought or feeling, but where it is expressed without restraint. The Church of Christ is a universal brotherhood. It recognizes no distinction of nation, race, or color. Whatever rules politicians may adopt with regard to trade, its commerce is free and its sympathies are unrestricted. The American Church has ever thrown open its doors to Christian pilgrims from every land, and liberally responded to every legitimate appeal for aid. France, England, Scotland, Ireland —the richest and most cultivated countries of the world—have not deemed it disgraceful to ask and receive its offering. Shall *it* alone be too proud to ask or receive? Shall it alone permit the interests of Christ's kingdom to suffer, and his poor to perish, from a false and pitiful spirit that will not brook the confession of want?

It may, indeed, be galling to the people of this great Christian Republic, after their grand revolt against the tyranny of Britain, and all their proud boasts of freedom, to be obliged to publish there, that an eminent minister of Christ, well known by his works in all the churches, has been ostracized, persecuted, and almost driven from his post, in consequence of his faithfulness and courage in denouncing an unparalleled system of oppression and wrong, maintained and defended by their government and laws. We do not wonder that an attempt should be made to impair the force and pungency of this terrible fact, by the pretended discovery of some apology for this wickedness in the spirit or manner with which this awful battle against the sin of slaveholding has been conducted. But it is vain. The severity of Dr. Cheever is the severity of truth; his sternness the sternness of justice; his hatred, a hatred of wrong. He has no bitterness. A kinder heart never beat. The tremendous energy and prophet-like fidelity with which he proclaims the denunciations of God's word against oppression *spring from the very depth and intensity of his love to God and man.* It is a shame that a man so meek, gentle, and unselfish in all the walks of life, and so regardless of his own reputation or interest in his public career, a man ever ready to throw himself into the gap to defend the truth at whatever cost, should be charged with the want of genuine kindness.

Nor will a reference to the popularity of eminent clergymen who profess anti-slavery principles avail. We admit that they are opposed to the system of slavery, and would rejoice to see it abolished. But do they believe in the inherent sinfulness of slaveholding, and would they exclude the slaveholder from the Christian Church, just as they would the habitual perpetrator and upholder of any other flagrant vice? As a class we have abundant evidence to compel us to reply in the negative. They do not and will not lay the ax at the root of the tree, by preaching against the sin of slaveholding. They will tell you that slavery in the world will last for ages; that the low, animal condition of the negro enslaves him, or at least justifies his continuance in bondage for a time; that the African race have not yet reached their spring time, and must be left to the influence of national freedom, and the slow process of those moral and intellectual forces which *may* reach them under all the terrible disadvantages of their condition, for the discovery of their manhood and the assertion of their rights. They attack the evils of slaveholding, and not the *radical sin* itself. They are very gentle to the Southerners, and would hold them affectionately to their hearts, and we see no reason why they should not do so *in a perpetual embrace.* There is scarcely a slaveholder who pretends to the decencies of religion who would not readily subscribe to every one of these principles. But let them hear the report of a single gun from the logic of the word of God against slavery as man-stealing, and they would fall back in a moment, and with indignant and defiant air, upbraid them as fanatics and madmen, and no blandness of manner or sweetness of tone would win them back to courtesy, much less to friendship.

There is another point of contrast between the anti-slavery ministrations of Dr. Cheever and those of his brethren, which sheds much light upon the different degrees of favor with which they are received. Dr. Cheever has grappled with the subject. He has pursued it through all its ramifications, and discussed it with a thoroughness and elaborateness which its own intrinsic importance, and the condition of the American Church and nation with regard to it, imperatively demanded. He has met the aggressions and development of the slave-power, whether they have appeared in the form of Congressional legislation, decisions of courts, or acts of ecclesiastical bodies, with the opposing testimony and burning denunciations of the word of God. The Fugitive Slave bill, the Dred Scott decision, the treachery of the American Tract Society, and the American Board, have in turn felt the withering power of his faithful rebuke. Indeed, so numerous and repeated have been his blows, that during the last few years the general impression has been that he was absorbed in the subject, though we who enjoy the privilege of sitting under his ministry, and, therefore, have a right to judge, do solemnly declare our belief, that, within this period, he has presented from the pulpit as great a variety of rich, profound, original, and profitable thought, on purely spiritual themes, as any minister in the United States. Now, no one, we think, will pretend that any other minister connected with the orthodox churches has put forth his strength against slavery in a similar degree, or has manifested any thing like the same anxiety or purpose for its immediate and entire abolition by the power of divine truth.

It will be seen by the statement we have made, that neither the Church of the Puritans, nor the Board of Trustees, have the slightest responsibility in this matter. We did believe that when the time came for laying it before the Church, a majority would sanction it; and now that it has been thrust upon us prematurely, and every kind of effort is put forth to increase our embarrassment, we have not lost our confidence. We can not think that the spirit of infatuation could so far take possession of our brethren as to allow them to lose sight of the mighty principles for which we are contending, and after all our struggles, sacrifices, and triumphs, to murder our own cause, and give back our noble citadel to the enemy, in consequence of some trifling differences of opinion respecting a measure admitted on all sides to have been well intended, in a time of great difficulty. But if we should prove to be mistaken on this point, however deep would be our regret, we would not despair, *much less would we withdraw our appeal. On the contrary, we should be obliged to urge it on with greater earnestness, for then we should not only require funds to enable us to carry on a church, but also to build one.* On this the nation and the whole world may depend, that, God helping us, the light which he has kindled here shall not be put out. In our hearts we believe it essential to the salvation of the Church and nation. Every body knows that Dr. Cheever is one of the ablest champions of the cause of freedom that has ever appeared, and is wielding at this moment a mighty influence throughout the country. God has said that he would never leave his Church without a witness. History will recognize him in this light. Why should not we?

We trust that the Christian abolitionists of New-York will no longer stand by and see him deserted, reviled, broken down inch by inch, struggling against fearful odds, but will rally at once, and in a body, to his support. We trust that in the light of this great cause they will perceive the utter insignificance of all those ordinary excuses based upon church ties, associations, friendships, family preferences, distances; and that, remembering those solemn words of Jesus, "He that loveth father or mother, husband or wife, brother or sister, houses or lands, more than me, is not worthy of me," they will now come forth and stand up for him in the true sense of that memorable charge, as it fell from the lips of the dying Tyng, by standing up for the enslaved, and by standing up for the great standard-bearer entrenched on Union Square, to whom that young hero pointed in the last speech he ever made on a platform in this city, and said: "If he be sustained, then no clergyman in this land shall have cause to fear!"

Christian abolitionists throughout the United States! the Church of the Puritans is a national church. God has made it so. It is a citadel of strength and power for you. The great truths uttered there, in the heart of the metropolis, are carried on the wings of the Press throughout the land. You have all read them and pondered them, and they have given you courage and hope. But you have not known till now the mighty troubles and sacrifices it has cost to maintain it. We have reached a crisis. Will you consent that the slave power and all the powers of darkness shall shout over its downfall? Are you willing that Dr. Cheever should be driven out on account of his brave and faithful proclamation of divine truth, and his enemies return and take possession? No! Then we earnestly entreat you to show it by your works. We want at least $50,000 to meet an annual ground rent of $1500, and place it as nearly as possible on the foundation of a Free Church.

Signed in behalf of the authors of the appeal. HENRY A. HARTT.

Church resolution indorsing British Mission after hearing the statement of Dr. Hart:

After a lengthy discussion, the following resolutions were adopted by the Church, in the second of which reference is made, as will be seen, to the document which had just been read:

Whereas, Neither the Church, as a body, nor the majority of its members, nor the Trustees of the Society, were consulted previous to application made in March last by certain brethren of the Church to British Christians for pecuniary aid, it is manifest that none can be held responsible for the matter or the manner of that appeal but the individuals who made it, and who are now quite willing to bear that responsibility; but

Whereas, Some of the wealthiest men of the Church, and others, have entirely withdrawn their support from the ordinary expenses of the Society, while some of the Trustees, men of ability and sagacity, now openly declare their opinion that the Church and Society can not be sustained:

Resolved, That we, the Church of the Puritans, assembled for this purpose, by public notice from the pulpit, do hereby declare our full conviction of the propriety and necessity of such appeal for external aid.

Resolved, That the document read to this Church, signed by the brethren who authorized that appeal to British Christians for pecuniary aid, entirely exonerates those brethren from all blame in the premises, and is hereby declared to be the deliberate judgment of this Church as to the present condition of the Society, and a truthful statement of the several steps by which that condition has been reached.

Resolved, That a copy of these resolutions, with the document above named, be forwarded to the Rev. Dr. Candlish, of Edinburgh, and the Rev. C. H. Spurgeon, of London.

Dr. BACON then called upon some of the complaining members to give their statements of the facts in relation to the British Aid Mission.

DR. G. H. WHITE'S STATEMENT.

Dr. White said, the first intimation that was received that Miss Johnstone was collecting money in England for the Church of the Puritans, was by a flying rumor. This rumor was boldly contradicted and branded as false by an article in the *N. Y. Independent*, to which paper Dr. Cheever was at that time contributing. With that the matter rested until the appearance of the Spurgeon Letter. As was my custom, I took up my daily paper one morning, and the first paragraph almost which attracted my attention was a comment by the *Times* editor, on this letter, which it stated had been published in England, and was republished in that morning's copy. I first read the editorial, saying to myself all the time: "No such letter was ever written by the Pastor of the Church of the Puritans."

I passed from the editorial to the letter, and read it in the hearing of my wife, repeating again and again the declaration: "Dr. Cheever never wrote this letter." But getting nearer the end, I began to believe that he must have written it, or some one who was perfectly familiar with his style. I could not bear the thought that he had written it. I said to myself, it would alienate him from the affections of the Church. That was the starting-point of my separation from Dr. Cheever, for I went to that Church to sustain him as an anti-slavery man—because he was an anti-slavery man—to battle with him against slavery, and I know that others went there for the same purpose who sided with me against the British Aid Mission.

Immediately on reading that letter through, and being convinced that it must have been written by Dr. Cheever, without consultation with a single individual, I wrote a resolution for the purpose of presenting it to the Church, calling upon the Church to repudiate such a mission as that being carried on. I wrote a resolution, and showed it to one sister and one brother of the Church before the evening meeting. I put the resolution in my pocket, and taking it to the meeting, at the close of the devotional exercises I arose and said: "I have an item of business which I wish to bring before the Church, and as by our rules we can not act upon it until another meeting, I will read it." The purport of it was the same as embodied in the action of the trustees at a subsequent sitting of that body. I intended to bring it up at the next weekly meeting. It so happened that at the time of the next meeting I was so ill that I could not be present, and I can not therefore speak of the course of proceedings at that meeting.

From the first development of that mission I have been opposed to it, because I believe that in the manner of its induction and in the course of its execution it was subversive of our Congregational polity—it struck at the roots of our Congregational system, it struck at our independence as a Christian church—it reached forth to an absolute domination of the Church by a few individuals. The simple fact that this brother or that brother would offer to get money and help in a righteous cause was of small consequence to me. That never raised a prejudice in my mind, and I cared not because it was British gold sought, but it was the manner of its inception, and the manner of its progress and its probable results that settled my mind to oppose it from the start, and which has actuated me from that time to this.

Dr. Ball's Statement.

Dr. Ball being called upon, said: The subject of this Spurgeon letter did not strike me at the meeting to which Mr. White refers as it did him. We had been through with a hard battle previously, and we thought we had secured rest and quiet to the Church. I feared now that we were to enter upon another conflict, and I felt very much opposed to it, and was at the time very desirous that we should not have any trouble about this subject. But I must say that I had not examined the matter in all its bearings upon the Church. But when the subject came out fully, and when it was revealed to us how this matter was commenced, and when it came out that the money was to be put into the hands of Dr. Cheever and two or three individuals of the Church, who were to be selected by Dr. Cheever, and were to hold it as a fund to support Dr. Cheever while he should preach according to the opinions—the anti-slavery beliefs of this committee—then I took ground against this movement, because I saw that it was subversive of the highest interests of the Church; that it would be utterly impossible that any pastor could be sustained by a church, while he was supported in that way. I had been there for six or eight years; I was anti-slavery in my feelings from my youth; I sustained Dr. Cheever because he was an anti-slavery preacher, and because I loved his ministry, and because I thought the subject of slavery should be preached on more or less. But when it came fully out that he was to be sustained in this way, I began then to think and see that it was a measure that would alienate the Church from him.

Rev. Dr. Dutton. How does it appear that this money was to be in the hands of Dr. Cheever and a few others?

Dr. Ball. That was the proposition. The question was asked, What was to be done with this fund? and the brother who commenced this movement, Dr. Hartt and others, replied, and this statement came out. Before this a number of us were disposed to get along with this thing if we could; but when this was made clear, I for one opposed it. Even to the present day there has no other disposition been made of this fund. The Church do not know where it is. They are ignorant as a body of what has been done with it. The matter was very thoroughly and earnestly discussed at one meeting of the Church at that time—the meeting continued almost all night—and it was not claimed that there was to be any other disposition of the money than that which has been stated.

This British mission was almost without exception opposed by every body in the Church. Most of those now sustaining it, state that when it was first propounded to them by Dr. Hartt, they were opposed to it. Even Dr. Cheever, himself, admits that when first propounded to him he was opposed to undertaking it. And the Church indorsed it, at a church-meeting, by a small majority, more from the desire to secure peace, if possible, to the Church, than from any conviction of the policy or justice of the movement.

Mr. Bennet's Statement.

Mr. Bennet being called on, said: I was chairman of the meeting at which the resolutions indorsing the British Aid Mission were passed. It was a very lengthy meeting, and there was a very full discussion of the subject, not always in the very best temper. Dr. Cheever appeared in the meeting, and took a very decided part, and urged very earnestly the necessity of the Church making some expression that would indorse the action that the self-constituted committee had seen fit to take on behalf of the Church. Most of the leading brethren of the Church, as far as I could judge from the discussion, and from what I knew of their opinions, were opposed to this English mission. It had been sprung upon us, and most of us, especially those who were in the Church for the purpose of sustaining the anti-slavery gospel that was being faithfully proclaimed by the pastor, thought we were about to be made slaves of, and we did not like it. We thought that our rights were being trespassed upon, and we did not feel pleasantly under it.

The Moderator.—Was it understood that the funds raised in England were to be controlled by a board of trust appointed by Dr. Cheever or otherwise, than by the Church?

Mr. Bennet.—Yes, sir. That fact was developed in the discussion.

Mr. Bennet proceeded to give an incident in Dr. Cheever's conduct on the evening of the meeting.

Dr. Thompson objected to any personal comments upon Dr. Cheever in his absence; but after explanation, the Moderator allowed Mr. Bennet to proceed.

One of the brethren was speaking, and made some remark in reference to the younger members, which called Dr. Cheever very suddenly to his feet, to read a private note that this same brother had written some time before to a confidential friend, in which he had alluded to the younger members of the Church as taking a part in business proceedings that was not quite proper. The object seemed to be to prejudice the influence of the brother who had been speaking, in his argument, to the youthful members. I called him to order, but not before he had read too far, for before allowing him to read a private note, I should have inquired into its character. I thought the note one exceedingly improper to be introduced, at the time, merely for the purpose of changing votes.

Rev. Dr. Thompson.—Would the reading of that confidential note have had an influence to make the young persons present cast their votes on the side of the pastor?

Mr. Bennet.—I think it would have had that influence. It was read unquestionably with that intention. Dr. Cheever did not deny that he read it with that intention. He felt himself justified, he said, in reading it. The note had providentially fallen into his hands, and he was justified in using it. I afterwards privately labored with him for some time, and told him he could not justify himself for reading the note, and I told him it was but proper that he should make an explanation to the aggrieved brother. He said if any one felt aggrieved, let them come to him and state their grievances. I asked him to point me to any Gospel requirement that would prevent his going and explaining the matter to the brother, and trying to reconcile him. He said he did not know that there was any objection to it, but he did not feel that it was his duty to do it.

For the resolution, as it passed, indorsing the British Mission, there was only a bare majority. The meeting was protracted so long, too, that I think a good many had left before the vote was taken.

A portion of an article from the *National Anti-Slavery Standard*, was here read, entitled, "Official Reply of the Church of the Puritans," as follows:

Extract from the Report of a Committee of the Church, published in the *New-York Anti-Slavery Standard*, Aug. 4th, 1860:

If they had not been so oppressed with the "swarms of locusts," and had ventured to examine the numerous documents, they would have learned that all the principal facts which they mention had been faithfully recorded for the benefit of the British people. The ground rent of $1500, the $22,000 required to meet it; the $50,000 or $100,000 desired to establish our noble citadel upon the foundation of a free church, where all might come without restraint, from North and South, East and West, rich and poor, slave-master and abolitionist, Democrat and Republican, saint and sinner, to hear the doctrines of primitive Christianity from the lips of an earnest and faithful man of God, all this was stated frankly and without reserve. But we did not say that American securities were worthless, or that the money we might procure ought to be invested in a sinking fund, and would most probably be lost.

We did not promise to consult our anxious friends, the clerical Rothschilds, and therefore had no fear. Nor did we deem it necessary to explain the law in relation to the constitufion and powers of the Society, *for we had not the remotest idea of placing the funds we might obtain in their hands. We did not even propose to commit it to the charge of the Church*, though, as at present constituted, we have unbounded confidence therein; *for who can tell what changes may occur?*

At the same time, as we wish to be frank, even to a fault, in this matter, we have no hesitation in saying, that there were other considerations which impelled us to the course we adopted. Our great object in applying to British churches for aid, was to raise a fund, *not to support the Church of the Puritans, or any other church as a mere ecclesiastical organization*, but to sustain the ministry of Dr. Cheever, free and untrammelled, in this edifice, if possible, if not, then in some other. We had no doubt at the time that a majority of the Church would sanction the appeal, if all the facts of the case were laid before them. But we knew that it would be an exceedingly difficult task, under existing circumstances, to present those facts to them in the same clear light in which they appeared to us, or in a form which would give them their legitimate influence. We were also aware that a large and influential minority, from the nature of the case, would bitterly oppose the measure. Besides, we had not been unobservant spectators of the manifold changes, defections, and desertions which had taken place in our midst, nor were we entirely ignorant of the fact, that in our own party we had men of the stamp of our good brother B——, men of eminent piety, rich in spiritual experience, assimilated in a high degree to the image of God, yet who, in one point of resemblance, signally fail. I allude to that great attribute referred to in the passage which says, with Him "is no variableness, neither shadow of turning." You will not wonder then we felt some doubt with regard to the permanence of our majority, and that we declined to ask the Church to engage in collecting, and consequently to assume the control of a fund which, by some not improbable changes in the views of individuals and the relations of parties, might be used for the very opposite purpose from that for which it was raised, or not used at all.

The following documents were then read, being the credentials furnished Miss Johnstone—her two agreements with Dr. Hartt, and extracts from various letters sent her after her departure:

NEW-YORK, February 28th, 1859.

TO THE CHURCHES OF CHRIST IN GREAT BRITAIN AND IRELAND:

DEAR BRETHREN: The Church of the Puritans in this city, under the pastoral care of the Rev. George B. Cheever, D.D., has, for several years past, been engaged in a deadly conflict with the sin of slavery. In 1850, immediately after the passing of the infamous Fugitive Slave Bill, the pastor delivered a discourse on that act, denouncing it from the word of God as an outrage upon natural rights, and subversive of the fundamental principles of morality and religion. So deep was the general apathy at that time, both in Church and State, that his burning words fell upon the congregation like a thunderbolt from a cloudless sky. The murmurs of dissatisfaction were loud and long, and one of the prominent members of the Church had the impious effrontery to demand of him what right he had to differ from the great constitutional lawyer and statesman, Daniel Webster?

Afterwards, the aggressive and rapicious spirit of the slave-power, by the removal of ancient landmarks and trusted safeguards of freedom, sent a thrill of alarm even through the heart of hoary expediency, and Dr. Cheever thought the time had come for striking a second blow. Accordingly, on Thanksgiving-day, 1855, he preached with great earnestness and force against the crime of oppression, and it was announced the next morning in one of the leading journals, that he appeared to see nothing before the country but desolation and woe. On this occasion, the impulsive brother above referred to was so intensely moved, that he was compelled suddenly to rise from his pew and leave the church. And now a spirit of disaffection broke forth, which no art could allay without a compromise of principle. It was seen that the pastor was profoundly impressed with the unspeakable wickedness of slavery, and had formed a stern and immovable purpose to open upon it all the batteries of the word of God. The cotton-brokers of the congregation and the worshipers of the pew-revenue were terrified beyond measure, and began forthwith to plot for the overthrow of this arch enemy of the interests of commerce and the prosperity of the Church. Undisturbed by their devices, however, he bravely persisted.

The discourses delivered at this time were afterward embodied in a volume published by Dr. Cheever, entitled, *God against Slavery*. At length a band of twenty conspirators engaged in a formal attempt to remove him from his post, but failing therein, they withdrew with their families from his ministration.

Meanwhile, as you may imagine, no small uproar was excited *without* the walls of the Church. The slave-power was justly alarmed. Hitherto the Church in this country had been silent, or given its testimony only in a passing rebuke, or in general resolutions adopted at conventions, as a quietus to conscience, and filed away for historical reference, that posterity might find *under the bushel the light which, in a spirit of blindness and apostasy, had been willfully excluded from the candlestick.* The battle for freedom has been carried on, for the most part, by men of noble nature, whose hearts instinctively revolted from the injustice and cruelty of slavery, and who, misled by the interpretations by which the testimony of the Bible on this point has been so sadly perverted, have rejected the great truth of its plenary inspiration, and thus deprived their argument of the omnipotence of its divine authority, and encumbered their cause with all the odiousness and opprobrium of infidelity. The convenient answer to all their noble utterances in behalf of human rights was, that they were the ravings of Unitarians and Pantheists. At length it came to pass that some of the plainest elementary principles of Christianity, when applied to this subject, were either evaded or denied, and a system of oppression unequaled in criminality and horrors since the world began, was fast coming to be enshrined in the national conscience, and transfigured by the Church into a glorious *missionary institution.*

It can not, therefore, be a matter of surprise when Dr. Cheever came forth as a minister of Christ, and in his name, and by his authority, denounced it as a mystery of iniquity and the sum of all villainies, utterly repudiated by the word of God, and worthy only of the divine vengeance, that the fountains of the great deep should be broken up, and all the waters of this ocean of abominations should be let loose upon him to overwhelm and destroy him. It is not necessary, dear brethren, that we should enter into a minute detail of the trials and persecutions which he has had to encounter in this tremendous conflict. You can readily imagine the storm which would at once assail him, both from the religious and a great portion of the secular press. You can easily picture to yourselves the desertion, the ostracism, the reproaches, the detractions of the clergy, and the general condemnation and reprobation of the Church. You will have no difficulty in fancying the outcry which would be raised against him as a political preacher, and the revival of the old epithet of fanatic and madman. It is a source of deep thankfulness that he has not been utterly discomfited and beaten down. His courage, indeed, rises with every new danger, and opposition only seems to quicken and invigorate both his intellectual and spiritual forces. His Church, though greatly weakened, still stands firm, and all we need to place us beyond the reach of our adversaries is pecuniary aid.

Under these circumstances, dear brethren, we appeal to you. We know your intense hatred of all oppression. We know the deep interest you feel in the African race, and the mighty efforts and sacrifices you have made on their behalf. We recognize the proud position in which your nation stands before the world, with an empire on which the sun never sets, untrod by the foot of a slave. Our hearts exult in this grand preëminence, because we ascribe it to the benign and sacred influence of our common Christianity, and because we see in it an earnest of our own deliverance and exaltation. Dr. Cheever has caught the inspiration of your own great confessors and martyrs of liberty. He is marching in the footsteps of Wilberforce, and Clarkson, and Buxton, and Gurney, and Thompson, and Wardlaw, and Knibb, who, in their day, unfurled the banner of divine truth and love, and led on the Church and nation to a glorious victory. We regard him as a witness raised up by the Almighty to our Church and nation. Endowed with a marvelous genius, furnished with the resources of an elaborate culture, eminently gifted with the graces of the Spirit, and prepared by a peculiar course of discipline, we could scarcely imagine a man more fitted to be a leader in this great cause. Nor can we fail to admire the Providence which has placed him, in this momentous crisis, on the most conspicuous site of this metropolis, the central tower in the land. The importance of sustaining him in this position can not be over-estimated. His overthrow would strike a blow at the freedom of the pulpit, and the freedom of man in this country, the disastrous effects of which no language could describe. On the other hand, his continuance there will enable him to hurl forth the thunderbolts of God's word with ever-increasing energy and power, and will give strength and courage to others, both among the clergy and the private members of Church, to follow his example. Already we begin to see the results of his labors, and we are persuaded that the candle which he has lighted in this land will never be put out, but will burn brighter and brighter, until it shall reveal to the hearts and consciences of the whole nation the true and full meaning, and universal application, of the famous declaration, "that all men are born free and equal, and have an inalienable right to life, liberty, and the pursuit of happiness;" and the insufferable infamy of the decision recently pronounced by the highest functionary in our supreme Tribunal of Justice—that "negroes have no rights which white men are bound to respect."

HENRY A. HARTT, M.D., } *Members of the Prudential Committee.*
D—— F——,
E—— F——,
E—— G——,
H—— S——, and others.*

NEW-YORK, February 28th, 1859.

I hereby certify that Miss Elizabeth Johnstone is a most esteemed and respected member of the Church of the Puritans in this city, of which Church I am pastor. Miss Johnstone visits Great Britain on a mission connected with the interests of this Church, in consequence of the desperate crisis through which we are passing in the great conflict for the rights and liberties of the oppressed colored race in this nation. We need aid, and we must have it; by the divine blessing we shall have it; and we commend Miss Johnstone, in any appeal which she may have opportunity to make, most cordially and respectfully to the friends of the slave, and of those who have been declared, by the inhuman judicial decisions of the Supreme Tribunal of our country, to have no rights that white men are bound to respect.

GEORGE B. CHEEVER.

FIRST AGREEMENT.

NEW-YORK, March 1st, 1859.

Miss Elizabeth Johnstone has undertaken to visit Great Britain, for the purpose of procuring funds for the benefit of the Church of the Puritans in this city. The money so obtained is to be given to Dr. Cheever, and a committee of not less than five members of the Church to be chosen by him, with power to appoint their successors, whose duty it shall be to make a good and safe investment thereof, and appropriate the interest towards the maintenance of the said Church, so long as it shall continue to uphold those great principles of freedom which it now so signally represents in the eyes of the whole world; and who, in the event of the abandonment by said Church of those principles, shall be empowered and required to devote both principal and interest to the establishment and maintenance of another Church of like principles, or some auxiliary object, as in their judgment and consciences may seem best.

HENRY A. HARTT, M.D.,
E. JOHNSTONE.

JESSIE HARTT, } *Witnesses.*
LYDIA M. MORE,

SECOND AGREEMENT.

Miss Elizabeth Johnstone has undertaken to visit Great Britain for the purpose of procuring funds for the Church of the Puritans in this city. The money so ob-

* Some of the names in this document have been suppressed for prudential reasons.

tained is to be given to Dr. Cheever, and a committee of not less than five members of the Church, with power to appoint their successors, whose duty it shall be to make a good and safe investment thereof, and appropriate the interest to the maintenance of the said Church, as long as it shall continue to uphold those great principles of freedom which it now so signally represents in the eyes of the whole world. The understanding with regard to the remuneration of Miss Johnstone for her services is, that she shall receive ten per cent on all the sums she obtains; and that she shall pay her own expenses; and that she takes upon herself all the risks of the enterprise.

(Signed) HENRY A. HARTT, M.D.

NEW-YORK, March 1st, 1859.

A copy of the above, it is believed, Dr. Hartt has in his possession, fully signed.

Additional sentences received by Elizabeth Johnstone, about the 13th of May, 1859, to strengthen her position:

STATEMENT RESPECTING THE CHURCH OF THE PURITANS.

Dr. George B. Cheever, Pastor of the Church of the Puritans in the City of New York, is well known in Great Britain as the author of *Lectures on the Pilgrim's Progress*, *Wanderings of a Pilgrim*, etc. He has been engaged for several years past in a deadly conflict with the sin of slavery, and is now recognized in his own country as the leading champion of the anti-slavery cause.

He has taken high ground. Instead of contenting himself with opposing the extension of slavery, and discussing the moral duties arising out of its existence, ... he lays the axe at the root of the tree, denounces slavery as sin, and brings all the artillery of God's word to bear against it; he earnestly longs and labors for its *immediate* and *utter extinction.*

He has long been regarded as one of the master minds in the country. When, therefore, he commenced his onslaught upon slavery, the attention of the nation was turned upon him. It was known that his blows would be tremendous, and would never cease till he or the monster should die. His Church at this time was in a most flourishing condition. The congregation was large, and the pew revenues abundant.

The Church stands in the very center of the metropolis, surrounded by the mansions of the fashionable and the wealthy. It promised, in the language of some who have since deserted it, to be a most successful enterprise; but no sooner was cotton, the great idol of the nation, attacked, than a dark cloud began to gather over the turrets of the temple on Union Square. The sword of the Spirit puts to flight the peace of a compromising Christianity. A fierce discussion broke forth, and after a desperate struggle, the Pastor triumphed. But a large body of the wealthiest and most influential members of the Church, including all the Deacons, forsook him, united with his foes, and have done all they could, by slander and misrepresentations, to break him down. A new conspiracy has since been formed, and at this moment there are men of wealth and power in the Church who desire his removal, and who would gladly avail themselves of the first opportunity to accomplish it.* The majority may be confidently relied upon, but they need

* Of this new conspiracy in the Church, I knew nothing until put in possession of this document; and even then I was not made aware of its nature.—E. J.

material aid to defray the inevitable expenses of the Church. There is a ground-rent upon the church of $1500 per annum, which is equivalent to a permanent debt of nearly $22,000.

Meanwhile, the whole force of the slave-power, and of the great body of the American Church, is against us.

Dr. Cheever may justly be regarded as the Luther of America. Will British Christians suffer him to be overborne? . . . . The whole force of the slave-power is concentrated upon him, and his overthrow would be disastrous to all the interests of Christianity.

Now, remember that you have full authority to represent this cause, and proceed boldly, only taking care to prevent a premature denouement in this country. The more that comes spontaneously from the hearts of the British people, after the leading men are apprised of the facts, the better. . . .

New-York, July 16th, 1859.

My Dear Miss Johnstone: I fear you have been grieved and vexed at my long silence. I would have answered your last letter immediately after its reception, but an article had just appeared in the *Independent*, with reference to your mission, which, I feared, might seriously embarrass Mr. G. T. in the effort which he contemplates on the first of August. I therefore wrote a long letter to him, stating all the facts referred to in that article, as they occurred, and explaining to him the precise nature of the difficulties which gave rise to your mission. . . . I have been ever since so intensely occupied, that I could not find a moment to write. . . . I do not see how any one can fail to understand it, after the most cursory perusal of the documents which you at first carried with you. Mr. T. and his son-in-law seemed to comprehend it perfectly, and were willing at once to coöperate with you. . . .

I can not forget that it was in the British churches that I learned to look upon our present economy as a faith and repentance dispensation. The Church, indeed, every where seems to have lost sight of the true Christian philosophy—the beautiful combination of *faith* and *works*, inculcated by Christ and his apostles. It makes me sick at heart to hear of ministers, whose fame is in all the churches, higgling about minute details in a cause like that of Dr. Cheever, wishing to know the precise amount of his salary, and how many cents exactly the income of the Church falls below the expenditures. It is enough for such men as G. G. T. to know that God has at length given a Luther to America, and that the slave-power, with its eighteen hundred millions of dollars, and vast political influences, has concentrated all its force upon him, and threatens to crush him down. Their hearts are in full sympathy with the champion of freedom, and they can readily imagine that there may be strong reasons why, in the midst of the conflict, *all* the circumstances of his position, and the precise condition of his troops, may not be published to the world without reserve.

True wisdom is often shown in withholding, rather than revealing, when the case in question is comprehensive and complicated. If, now, we had postponed our efforts in behalf of Dr. Cheever, until we could have presented a full detail of the facts, we would have waited to have seen him thrust forth from the Church of the Puritans, defeated and trodden down; and then, amid the deafening yell of tyrants rejoicing over liberty prostrate, freedom of speech outraged, and the independence of the American pulpit trampled in the dust, with what patience and calmness we might, under such circumstances, have been able to command, we would have recounted the history of the conflict with the minutest particularity, and concluded with the significant and by no means poetical fact, that Dr. Cheever was without a church, with a few faithful but penniless followers, and required at least one hundred thousand dollars to renew the fight. Would that have been wisdom? Certainly not; for, in addition to all other evils, the disastrous moral influence of such a defeat could not be over-estimated. Yet that is precisely the course which those practically counsel who demand more definite statements. . . .

You may rely upon it, my dear Miss Johnstone, that I have not acted rashly in this matter, nor on my own judgment merely. Every step was carefully weighed, and nothing resolved upon without the entire concurrence of Dr. Cheever, whom I regard as unquestionably the master-mind of America.

We were by no means sure of your success. . . . We did hope they would respond cordially to our appeal. If they have not done so, it is not *our* fault, nor *yours*. *We* have done *all* that under existing circumstances was *possible*.

You must not be affected by any thing you may see in any of the American papers. As yet we have no organ, There is, therefore, nothing published in any of the journals that may be relied upon as exclusively ours. . . . We hope now to have a true paper in this city.

I have nothing new to write. The world moves of course, and so do we. But nothing has transpired that particularly affects your mission. I think you would do well to explore a little among the Dissenters. They used to be warm friends of freedom.

Can you not get Dr. G. at work? Now, my dear friend, I commend you to God and the word of his grace. If he smile upon our undertaking, it will prosper. I am sorry that Dr. Cheever can not go over. His new work detains him. I am much grieved at your annoyances and disappointments, but I trust a brighter day will soon dawn.

Ever yours, most truly, H. A. Hartt.

FRIDAY MORNING SESSION.

In answer to questions as to certain dates, Dr. Thompson said:

On the 10th of January, 1859, I was invited to the house of Dexter Fairbank, to join in the presentation to Dr. Cheever of a testimonial of $1000. About the same time a subscription was inaugurated, binding, on condition the whole required amount should be subscribed, to free Dr. Cheever's Church from debt. In a few weeks, it was said that enough had been pledged to put the Church out of debt, and the subscriptions were collected. I rejoiced to learn that the Church was financially safe; yet, all the while this British Aid movement was secretly going on; for the date of the letter given Miss Johnstone is February 28th, 1859.

In May, 1859, the *Anti-Slavery Advocate*, in London, noticed the presence of Miss Johnstone making these collections. I saw the statement in June, when away from the city. I wrote a hasty paragraph for the *Independent*, stating that, within a few months this Church had given its Pastor $1000, and had paid off all its debts, and therefore this could not be true. I thought, in all honesty, it was a scandal. This was the paragraph which some of the brethren of the Church saw, and which set them at rest. Being at Norwich, I did not see Dr. Cheever before writing the paragraph, and he did not afterwards contradict it. The facts given in that article as to the financial ability of the Church, were all correct.

Miss JOHNSTONE said it was fully six weeks after the proposition was made to her that the arrangement was perfected. It was finally arranged in February that she was to go. Some time elapsed between the proposition being accepted and her departure.

MR. ALLEN'S STATEMENT.

Mr. WILLIAM ALLEN being called upon, said:

I was Chairman of the Board of Trustees in 1858 and 1859, or for three years ending April 1st, 1860. For these three years the congregation fell off very much, and the revenues had also fallen off. About a week preceding the 1st of January, 1859, Dr. Hartt and Dr. Cheever called on me to broach to me the project they had formed, to obtain subscriptions to pay for the debts of the society. They suggested two ways to do it. They said that there were some who were willing to contribute to pay the debts of the society directly, and others would not, but would contribute to Dr. Cheever personally. It was therefore proposed that they carry on two subscriptions, one towards paying the debt of the Society, and the other as a compliment to Dr. Cheever. It was understood, however, that what Dr. Cheever received was to be given to the same purpose as the other subscription; he was to take the responsibility of appropriating it to that purpose. The express object for collecting these funds before the annual meeting of the Church, was, that it might appear to the public that the Society was prosperous—that it was not running down. I objected decidedly to collecting a testimonial to Dr. Cheever, on the ground that it was the duty of the congregation to pay their debts before they should raise an amount of money for the Pastor personally. The object was distinctly held up, that it would not do to have the impression go out that the society was not prospering. At the annual meeting, about the second week in March, subscriptions had been pledged to about pay off the debt.

I knew nothing of the mission of Miss Johnstone until the appearance of the Spurgeon Letter. After the British Mission became public I resigned my place. I was so averse to church quarrels, that I would not stay in the Church to be identified with any church controversy. The Trustees had felt it to be their duty to take action on the subject.

It may be proper for me to say, that under the laws of the State the Society is incorporated, and the property is not subject to taxation. Now the Society has the charge of all the temporalities of the congregation, and if they have any functions at all it is to take care of the finances. The Trustees are the representatives of the Society; the title of the property is in them, just the same as the title of the property in a bank is in the directors. The Church has nothing to do with the property under the laws of the State; and if the Church, or any members of the Church, had undertaken to take the financial functions out of the hands of the Society, they usurped the functions of the Society — they violated the rights of the ecclesiastical Society. My objection to the action of these individuals was based on that ground — that they usurped the functions of the Society or Trustees, in secretly applying to a foreign community for a large fund.

Dr. Cheever, however, took the ground, that the Society and Trustees had nothing to do with it, and he stated to me that he thought it was an insult to him that they took any action on the subject. I replied that the Trustees found Dr. Cheever before the public, in the Spurgeon letter, and they were obliged to meet him where they found him. They had simply expressed their sentiments on the subject, without intending to be personal.

The object for which the subscription was taken was to keep up appearances before the public, because it was said that it would injure them not to be thought prosperous, and their enemies would send up a shout of triumph over their troubles.

Dr. Cheever made a very generous contribution towards paying off the debts of the Society of $600, which I think was stated to be from the proceeds of lectures.

Rev. Dr. Thompson.—To ascertain whether there was not real financial ability remaining in the congregation, to have supported the Gospel abundantly, if all things had been satisfactory, let me ask whether, about this same time, a *bona-fide* subscription of $3000 was not made in response to an appeal on behalf of the Congregational Union? And every subscription of this amount has been paid, I believe, with the exception of the subscriptions of two of the authors of the British Aid Appeal; and this was before the British Mission was known in the church. So it appears in the four months from January to May, there was given to Dr. Cheever a testimonial for $1000; there was raised a subscription of some $3500; and the Church contributed $3000 to the Congregational Union, and another $1000 was pledged towards the prospective expenses of another year. Is all this correct?

Mr. Allen corroborated this, and continued: The Church was built upon leased ground, and the rent of the ground is $1500. It was considered by Dr. Cheever very important that this location on Union Square should be retained. The ordinary expenses of the congregation would amount to about $5000. It had been, also, a custom with some of the brethren, to present the Pastor on the 1st of January, with a New-Year's compliment, which amounted usually to from three to five hundred dollars.

Rev. Dr. Budington.—I should like to get at the exact amount which the Church actually raised at that time.

Mr. Allen.—The amount is this: $1000 as a compliment to Dr. Cheever, $3500 to make up the debt for expenses, $3000 for the Congregational Union, and $1000 pledged for the coming year.

The statement of Miss Johnstone, of the British Aid Mission, was then read, as follows:

THE BRITISH MISSION.

A Report of the British Mission of the Church of the Puritans, being a statement of facts, financially and otherwise, as illustrating the course of the Church in regard to it.

Inasmuch as the British Mission, which I undertook in behalf of the Church of the Puritans, in February, 1859, was subsequently indorsed by said Church, in November of that year, when they, the Church, proposed resolutions in favor of this mission, and adopted them, I claimed it as a matter of right that I should be permitted to lay before the Church, not only a statement of some facts connected with this mission, which were not embodied in the pamphlet I published, for the reason that they were not quite relevant to the object I had in view in publishing that pamphlet, and from not then being in possession of sufficient information to say, with certainty, that deception had been practiced towards me from the first inception of the mission; but that I should be permitted to vindicate myself from those assertions made by Dr. Hartt, in the *New-York Times* of January 17th, 1861, by which he has impugned my veracity, and which, in the event of my not being well known in New-York and on the other side of the Atlantic, might have had the effect of destroying my position and reputation in society.

This right of having my report brought before the Church was twice denied me by the Committee under whose auspices the British Mission was conducted, and the Board of Trustees of the Church. I now seek another method by which to make known those facts, as illustrating the course of the Church in regard to this mission.

As has already been said in the pamphlet which I found necessary to publish—in order to remove misrepresentation that had been made in regard to my relation to, and course of action in, the prosecution of this mission—when I suggested the idea of appealing to Great Britain for aid, and offered my services for that purpose, it was because of certain representations made to me by Dr. Hartt, regarding the depressed financial condition of the Church; and that unless aid were speedily obtained, the Church *would and must* go down.

This condition of the Church, he informed me, was caused by a band of twenty conspirators, who, with their families, withdrew from the Church because they failed in their attempt to remove the Pastor; and that in consequence of this diminution in the church membership, the church revenue had fallen so low that it was insufficient to meet the wants of the Church. In the letter of appeal, under date February 28th, 1859, to the British Churches, with which I was sent forth to England, he reïterates the same thing. His words are as follows: "At length a band of twenty conspirators engaged in a formal attempt to remove him (the Pastor) from his post, but failing therein, they with their families withdrew from his ministrations. . . . His Church, though greatly weakened, still stands firm, and all we need to place us beyond the reach of our adversaries, is pecuniary aid. Under these circumstances, dear brethren, we appeal to you, etc. etc." Such were the statements made to me —such are the statements embodied in that letter of appeal—and on those statements alone I went to England and solicited aid to be appropriated according to the design set forth in my agreement. But let us see, in the light of subsequent information, which I am now in possession of, how far those statements of Dr. Hartt were correct.

Since my return home I have found that the Church was not in the depressed financial condition, as represented by Dr. Hartt to me, both previous and subsequent to the inception of the mission.

At a business meeting of the Church in April, 1860, I find that Mr. James O. Bennet, then a warm friend of Dr. Cheever, made the following statement, namely: "That previous to the appeal being made to England, in 1859, for aid, the Church had provided for all the wants of the Church. And he denied there was any occasion for sending to Great Britain at all for aid." I have also found that for the following current financial year, ending in April, 1860, twelve months after my arrival in England on this mission, and about four previous to my return home, '$10,657 had been collected and paid for the Church," (irrespective of any British aid.) Such is Mr. Berry's statement of the provision for the next or following year.

Now, inasmuch as the statements of the financial condition of the Church, made by Messrs. Bennet and Berry—then two of Dr. Cheever's warmest friends, and thorough anti-slavery men—entirely falsify Dr. Hartt's representations, which he made to me of the Church's financial condition, entirely falsify the statements which he made in the letter of appeal to the British churches, under date February 28th, 1859, as to the cause and necessity of that appeal, the question now arises, For what was this money wanted? For it is evident from the statement of Mr. James O. Bennet, and the report of the Board of Trustees, submitted by Mr. Berry, that the Church was self-sustaining during those two years at least, while I, for more than two thirds of that time, had been begging money, and having it sent out to keep the Church from going down, as Dr. Hartt termed it. Yea, my anxiety to obtain money in order to prevent this catastrophe was increased tenfold by the receipt of a letter from Dr. Hartt, under date 6th September, 1859, in which he reïterates the same statement, by saying: "The crisis approaches, and whatever can be done must be done without delay. And unless we get aid we must go down." Such is what he wrote to me in September, 1859, notwithstanding the Church had provided for all the wants of the Church for the financial year then past, and on the termination of the one then current $10,657 were collected and paid.

From the above statements I now fully understand why specifications as to the strength of the church membership; as to the income of the Church; as to how far the income of the Church fell below its expenditure, were not given when they were requested and pointed out by myself and others as being necessary. According to the statement of Mr. Bennet, and the report of the financial condition of the Church by Mr. Berry, those specifications could not be given. And I now also understand the full meaning of the following letter, which I received from Mr. Spurgeon, in reference to the necessity of the mission.

"Dear Madam: Upon consulting with my honored friend, Dr. C——, I am of his opinion, that you have not made out any case, and I am quite in the dark as to what the money is required for. According to an article which has been inserted both in English and American newspapers, there is clearly no need of funds in connection with Dr. Cheever's Church, and I must, therefore, positively decline moving in this matter until I hear from Dr. Cheever himself, and am able to see any need for funds at all.

"I rejoice in the Doctor's grand stand for liberty, but can not see any connection between that matter and your visit to England.

I am, yours, most truly,

Clapham, May 28th. C. H. Spurgeon."

According to subsequent developments, the Rev. Mr. Spurgeon was right, while there stood I, the victim of a crooked policy, occupying in my then ignorance a most questionable position, and one quite untenable, according to subsequent developments. Nothing but a conscientious belief in the correctness and tenability of my position could have carried me through the difficulties and discouragements of a similar nature that ever and anon crossed my path, little dreaming that I should make the discovery that it was because of a second conspiracy in the Church, whether suppositional or otherwise, to remove the Pastor; or that there was abundant power in the Church to sustain it, but that that power was in the hands of men who were anxious to use it for the Pastor's overthrow, that my proposition of this mission was entertained and accepted. These things, if they did exist, I left the shores of America in the most profound ignorance of. They never were communicated to me by Dr. Hartt, nor any one else previous to my entering on the British Mission. I had been engaged in the mission nearly two months and a half before I received the slightest intelligence of a *new* conspiracy, which, from the manner in which it was mentioned, in a document sent me when in England, I concluded had been discovered after my arrival in that country; and which, by its being so casually mentioned, as it were, and without any explanation whatever, I took no notice of in my prosecution of the mission, for the simple reason that I could explain nothing about it, and regarded it only as something in addition to the ostensible cause and necessity of the mission. But such I have discovered was not the case. For this conspiracy, which I believe existed in Dr. Hartt's brain only, from what I have recently heard fall from his lips at a church-meeting, in reference to Mr. Abernethy, was discovered by him in December, 1858, nearly three months before I undertook this mission; and which I have since learned was the cause that necessitated this mission, not the representations which he (Dr. Hartt) made to me of the Church.

Now, I ask, was this conduct of making representations to me of a condition of the Church which did not exist, and of taking the advantage of my credulity in those representations, by allowing me to go to England to seek for aid, while the real or supposed cause of the necessity for this aid was concealed, that of a straight-forward, honest man? With every impartial mind there can be but one opinion on the matter.

Dr. Hartt should be made to feel that he is not at liberty to play off such strokes of policy, which though he may for the present escape their consequences, yet to those who have been duped by them they may prove to be of deep and lasting injury.

Making an offer of my time and services to go to England to plead for what was represented to me a poverty-stricken Church, was one thing, but offering my time and services to plead for it, because of a conspiracy in it, was quite another. Had such been made known to me, I should have paused and made inquiries before offering my services under such circumstances.

It will avail Dr. Hartt, as principal manager in this matter, nothing, in extenuation for the injuries I have sustained through his crooked policy, to seize hold of—in addition to his concoction of my being desirous of visiting my friends as the reason why I was intrusted with this mission—the fact of my saying to one or two persons, but shortly before my departure, from the mission then being private, and not to be assigned as a reason of my voyage, that I was going to see my friends. This was true, as a *consequence* of the mission, not as a *motive*. The following extracts of a letter of Dr. Cheever to George Thompson, clearly settle this point, as well as that of the mission's being my proposition. These extracts are as follows:

NEW-YORK, June 28th, 1859.

MY DEAR FRIEND THOMPSON: . . . . From individuals we have received timely and encouraging aid. But in these circumstances, and just when our cause seemed almost desperate, Miss Johnstone thought she would present our cause to some friends in England, with a successful result. We did not lay this proposition before the Church, for it could not safely have been done. It would have become public, and excited a new discussion and dispute. . . . But a few gentlemen being consulted, agreed that there could be neither harm nor wrong in letting Miss Johnstone make this trial. We consented, and gave her what we supposed would be testimonials sufficient for operating in a quiet way. . .

Ever most truly and gratefully, yours,

GEORGE B. CHEEVER.

It is now well understood that I went to Great Britain on written agreement. I went for no extraneous purpose in connection with the Church of the Puritans, whether in contemplation or otherwise, but simply to solicit funds under the impression given, that the Church was not self-sustaining, and that the money so solicited, if obtained, was to be invested to meet a heavy ground rent. Such was the understanding, and so my agreement runs. But let us see how this agreement has been kept, and how I have been used in the matter.

Passing by altogether the intimation to me of a project of procuring a colleague for Dr. Cheever, after my arrival in Great Britain, with a request that I should embody it in the documents which it was expected I should draw up, being at variance with my agreement, I shall here first take up the request which was made by Dr. Hartt, that I should take care that all the moneys obtained should be presented to Dr. Cheever, himself, as a testimonial from the friends of freedom, and he to place them in the hands of those who could be relied upon for a right appropriation of them, in accordance with the design of the *donors*.

Now, inasmuch as the mode of appropriation of these moneys is clearly pointed out in my agreement, and inasmuch as Dr. Hartt, in his letter of the 26th April, informed me that he never intended that agreement to be used in England at all, except in a private way—though that was the first intimation I had of this (his intention)—leaving it entirely to the discretion of a few leading men to state its contents to their people or not, the design of the donors would not be in accordance with the design of that agreement, except in a few instances, if in any at all, therefore, the inference is, that the design of the donors would be in accordance with the representations, the requests, or the suggestions of those at head-quarters, irrespective of my agreement at all, and on which alone I undertook this mission. In this conclusion I am fully borne out on documentary evidence.

First. From the fact that a request was made in April, 1860, to the Rev. Dr. Johnston, of Edinburgh, that the collection from his Church should be applied to meet the expenses of publishing Dr. Cheever's last book, entitled, *The Guilt of Slaveholding; or, the Guilt of Slavery demonstrated from the Hebrew and Greek Scriptures*, in consequence of an interdict having been issued against it because of its sentiments, I think I was told.

On being put in possession of this information by one of the leading members of Dr. Johnston's Church, I sent him a copy of my agreement, with a few remarks on the matter. In his letter in reply to mine to him on the subject, he states that a letter had just been received by Dr. Johnston from Dr. Cheever, intimating that he and his people were obliged for the consent that had been given as to the application of the money.

Whom Dr. Cheever meant by his "people," I do not know, unless they were his Church. If so, I ask, did they inquire into the nature and terms of that agreement previous to their having adopted resolutions regarding it, which resolutions being adopted, the mission was by them indorsed? I rather think not. Otherwise they surely never would have consented to the breaking of that agreement without my knowledge. It is to be regretted that they, for their own credit, did not make inquiries previous to their indorsing the mission, as by this omission they have not only become a party to the breaking of an agreement for one of the most questionable purposes possible, but they have indorsed that part of it which would have required the serving of a double apprenticeship under the Merchant of Venice, to have devised and drawn up any thing more at variance with, and repugnant to the feelings and principles which characterize the man of humanity and equitable dealing; for it does not contain one single loop-hole through which I could have escaped to save myself from starving, had circumstances favored the realization of such a situation.

Perhaps Dr. Hartt, being aware of the disingenuous policy which he was at the time—at the eleventh hour—observing toward me, framed that agreement so; the risks of the mission from that policy being then in strong prospective.

It is my duty to inform the Church of the Puritans that the breaking of my agreement is not attended by any extenuating circumstances at all. On the contrary, the object to which the money, which had been collected for the Church of the Puritans, was now to be applied, should not, according to letters which I have in my possession, have existed.

According to these, letters which I have in my possession, relative to the whole of this matter, neither interdict nor injunction had been issued against Dr. Cheever's book, as represented to Dr. Johnston and his Church, when application was made that the contribution from his Church should be applied to meet expenses incurred by its publication; but simply an intimation that it was preferred that the book might be suppressed, in consequence of its publication being an *infringement of a copy-right*, held for one half of it, which was formerly published as articles in the *Bibliotheca Sacra.*

Now, so far from there being any necessity for the request of this money to be applied toward the defraying of the expenses incurred by the publication of this book, there was none. For W. F. Draper, of Andover, Mass., to whom belongs the copy-right, made overtures to Dr. Cheever to guard against loss in case of suppression, when he intimated his desire that the book might be suppressed.

Thus Dr. Cheever and his people had very little to be obliged for indeed, when they sent over that letter of thanks for the consent given by Dr. Johnston and his Church as to the application of that money.

As to the liberty which was taken with myself in this affair, I regard it as most high-handed and daring presumption. For not only was this money, which had been solicited and given for the Church of the Puritans, requested to be applied to the object above alluded to, but there were sent to me, while in Great Britain, prospectuses of the nature of the book, with a view to solicit subscriptions for its publication, thereby making me an aider and abettor in this discreditable affair, to say nothing of the not very pleasant position in which I now find myself by having sent a copy of it to the Queen of England, which was acknowledged July 4th, 1860.

In duty to myself I here disclaim all knowledge of any violation of a copyright of any part of that book, by its being published by Dr. Cheever, when I was soliciting subscriptions for its publication on prospectuses sent me, while in Great Britain, and which I circulated very extensively. It was only on the 6th of March, 1860, that I fully ascertained the facts regarding it, and only within three months since I received the first intimation about its publication being an infringement on Mr. W. F. Draper's copy-right, the facts of which are as follows: Mr. W. F. Draper, Andover, Mass., holds the copy-right for at least one half of the book, which half was published as articles in the *Bibliotheca Sacra*, for the years 1855 and 1856. To these articles, I am informed, Dr. Cheever added some other matter, and published his book. Mr. Draper, who paid for these articles $140, on seeing that Dr. Cheever's book was an infringement on his right, wrote to Dr. Cheever, informing him of this, and that he would prefer that the publication be suppressed, adding, that as he knew considerable loss would be sustained in case of suppression, he would, if Dr. Cheever desired to continue the publication, either sell his right or take a percentage on the copies sold. To this Mr. Draper never received any reply.

Still further with regard to my agreement, I am prepared to show that not only was the keeping of it but a secondary consideration with the New-York Committee, or perhaps, more properly speaking, with Dr. Hartt, but that there were other objects in contemplation to which the money I was soliciting was to be applied, besides the ostensible one for which alone I undertook this mission.

During my two months detention in Glasgow for the want of funds to take me home, I was put in possession of a part, in the form of a continuation of a letter, written by Dr. Hartt to George Thompson, London, which fully proves this statement, and from which the following is an extract:

The money would not be *lost*, *even* though we should recruit our ranks sooner than we anticipate, for we have before us, you know, a mighty work, requiring many agencies and a mine of wealth. After the thorough establishment of the Church of the Puritans on a solid foundation, we need an orthodox *Tribune*, a paper which shall represent Christianity, and honestly apply its principles to all the great questions of the day. Then will follow Church anti-slavery organizations, with a band of effective *lecturers*, and *multitudinous publications* for the indoctrination of the masses throughout the country. I can not tell you, my dear sir, how ardently I desire that you should aid us in this great enterprise. . . .

Yours, very truly, H. A. Hartt.

The same mail that brought this letter of date 25th and 26th November, 1859, to George Thompson, of which the above is an extract, brought one to myself, in which I was informed that it had been proposed to him that he should work in concert with me for six months in this mission. In the letter to myself the desire was expressed that the mission should be continued for six months longer. I had then labored nine in it, so that this six months longer was in addition to those nine. But in the letter sent to me I was not informed, as was George Thompson in his, that this six months' longer continuance of the mission was not to be exclusively for the object for which I undertook it, but also with a view to obtain money to aid in the carrying on of this great projected enterprise. This discovery I did not make until six months after George Thompson's receipt of the letter alluded to, when that part of it was sent me, from which the above is an extract, with an intimation that if there were any other letters or papers that would be of service to me, he would be happy to let me have them, therefore I feel quite at liberty to make use of this letter.

Without at all calling in question the desirableness of this enterprise, I ask, was this also what the Church of the Puritans indorsed when they adopted resolutions respecting my mission? Or was this straightforward dealing by me for that committee, under whose auspices this mission was conducted, to allow me to go to England in full belief that there was but one ostensible object for which I was to solicit aid, and then when there, and in full prosecution of the mission, to bring forward objects ulterior to this mission; nay, even projects for the consideration of other parties, thereby giving opportunity for the accusation of apparent inconsistency on my part in pleading one thing only as the object of my mission, while other parties were informed, not to the contrary, but that other objects, and even projects were in contemplation.

Being put in possession of that most important part of Mr. Hartt's letter to George Thompson, made me less regret my two months' detention in Glasgow for the want of funds to take me home, notwithstanding his assertion, on affidavit, "that as soon as he found that I needed money to take me home, it was promptly supplied," an assertion which is most false. For as early as the 18th of January, 1860, I sent to him a letter informing him to make arrangements for my return, and other purposes. This was more than five months previous to my being supplied with money to take me home. And when I was supplied with this money, it was neither by Dr. Hartt's orders nor by his sending it at that time, but by Mr. H. D. D., who gave me his check on the city of Glasgow Bank, he relying on being reïmbursed from New-York. That this money was not refunded as late as December 19th, 1860, the following extracts from a letter of Mr. H. D. D., a member of the Cheever committee in Edinburgh, will testify, notwithstanding the assertion of promptness by Dr. Hartt, as principal manager in this matter. These extracts are as follows:

EDINBURGH, 19th December, 1860.

MY DEAR MISS JOHNSTONE: I have received two letters from you. . . . I was glad that at our preliminary meeting he (Dr. Cheever) completely vindicated you from all the insinuations which had been thrown out, and also that you had been vindicated in New-York. Complete vindication and sympathy were certainly what you were entitled to. Your conduct was disinterested and heroic. You seem to expect that the money which was advanced to take you home will be refunded, and that a letter would be sent expressing the opinion and feelings on the whole matter; neither money nor letter has yet come. I would be very glad if such a letter were sent. . . . I am, my dear friend, yours sincerely, H. D. D.

That the crooked policy which Dr. Hartt observed, from the first inception of the mission and during its prosecution, was the cause of its want of entire success, these pages, with those of the pamphlet which I found necessary to publish, afford more than presumptive evidence. Yet I do not regret this, for, in the providence of God, perhaps it was a very good thing. For myself, individually, I feel this to be the case; and I am ready to bear, if need be, the sacrifice I made in relinquishing my annual average income of not less than $800; the loss of one year and four and a half months' time, with more than $600 which I gave toward the prosecution of the mission, rather than occupy a questionable position.

In undertaking and prosecuting the mission, I gave towards it, of my own money, $602.12. Mr. Fairbank and Mr. Hartt gave between them to aid it, $100, making in all $702.12. The amount spent as being immediately necessary to the carrying on of this mission was $677.88, irrespective of $30.76 for other expenses rendered necessary only by the mission's being prolonged so much beyond the time I intended to spend in it, so that in reality the total amount of money spent in, and in connection with this mission, was $708.64. The time occupied in undertaking and prosecuting this mission was one year four and a half months. Thirteen and a half months of that time were devoted to the most arduous and laborious exertions by which, notwithstanding all the obstacles and difficulties in the way, there were raised for the Church of the Puritans, $2638.96, exclusive of other promised moneys, in the shape of church collections and balances of former contributions, of which as yet I have received no information as to amount.

The moneys raised and collected through my exertions, and which have been officially advertised in British papers and British Anti-Slavery Society reports, are as follows:

Per Edinburgh Committee for Dr. Cheever,	£237	15	8½
Per Ladies' Emancipation Society, Edinburgh,	60	0	0
Per Rev. Dr. Johnston's Church, Edinburgh,	9	7	0
Per Rev. Mr. Kenton, Kelso,	30	0	0
Per Ladies' Anti-Slavery Society, England,	10	0	0
Per Lord Kinaird, Dundee, Scotland,	5	0	0
Per Glasgow Committee, Scotland,	40	0	0
Per Ladies' Anti-Slavery Society, Scotland,	12	0	0

Balance of Glasgow Committee's collections up till the end of October 1860, and handed to Dr. Cheever,..............	£100 0 0
Per Dr. Candlish's Church, one of two collections for the Church of the Puritans,..............................	27 13 3
Per Dr. Lindsay Alexander's Church, Edinburgh,..........	13 8 11½
Equal to $2638.98.	£545 4 11

As remuneration for my services I received $198.44. Of this sum there were $96.80 appropriated to defray expenses of the mission, and $101.64 to take me home.

This remuneration money of $198.44 being added to the sum $403.68, makes the sum of $602.12, mentioned as my own personal money, which was given to the undertaking and prosecution of the mission, as follows:

At the commencement of the mission in March, 1859, I gave, in sterling money,...	£41 0 0
In January and the spring of 1860, gave..................	33 16 6
Between the 19th and 25th March, 1860, gave,............	20 0 0
While in London in the last week of April, 1860,...........	8 11 8
And while in Glasgow, to take me home, I received,........	21 0 0
Equal to $602.12.	£124 8 2

The loss I have sustained by money spent in this mission, the loss of time and the sacrifice I made, to say nothing of other interests which have been destroyed by my prolonged absence, is not less than $1500. Rather too much indeed, seeing that neither the cause of the slave, nor the interests of humanity, nor those of Christianity can be benefited by an enterprise which I fear can not stand inspection in the light of developments which have since been made.

In the light of these developments I have now not the slightest hesitation in saying, that I was deceived from the first inception of this mission, as regarded the then true condition of this Church. Hence one reason why I was kept in ignorance of all that was transpiring at home. The whole affair I regard as of very grave character indeed. My proposition to appeal to England for aid ought never to have been entertained, much less accepted, if I could not have been made acquainted with the true condition of matters—the nature of the then existing difficulties—and this so-called conspiracy, which according to Dr. Hartt's own account—I was informed through a gentleman in England—discovered itself at a trustees' meeting. Dr. Hartt's conduct to me in regard to this matter, as well as his conduct in others, is highly reprehensible, and has been productive of deep and serious injury to me not only on this side of the Atlantic, but on the other.

Also the sending to me prospectuses with a view to my soliciting subscriptions to defray the expense of publishing Dr. Cheever's book, I regard as a most grave offense under the circumstances, and will here conclude by saying, If the cause of the slave, the great questions of the day, the multitudinous publications, and the band of effective lecturers are to be advocated, and the great principles of Christianity to be applied to them by such a *modus operandi* as that which the Church (?) of the Puritans is pursuing, then may she throw down the gauntlet for any moral power or spiritual life she possesses; nor may she ever again presume to plead the principles of common honesty, or the cause of the slave, until she herself has learned to be honest, has learned not to oppress.

Elizabeth Johnstone.

APPENDIX.

Since finishing my report I have been informed by the Committee of the British Aid Mission that they repudiate my account against the Church for printing, postage and stationery, incurred during eight months' prosecution of the mission, previous to the Edinburgh Committee's taking it up, on the ground that it is not based on agreement with Dr. Hartt. They also repudiate the additional remuneration that is due me, because it is not based upon the amount received by the Committee as the proceeds of my agency.

With regard to the first objection, I have to say, that Dr. Hartt distinctly told me that the Church would pay all expense for postage, stationery, and printing. Though such was not put in the agreement by him, there are parties in this city to whom he intimated the same thing.

With regard to the second objection, I have to say that my claim for additional remuneration is based upon my agreement, and the officially advertised amounts of money obtained by my exertions. With regard to my agreement, it reads, "She shall receive so much on all the sums she obtains," not on what the New-York Committee obtains or receives, after necessary expenses being deducted—but on what she obtains. This information which I have received from this Committee is in direct contradiction to my agreement; and also to that which Dr. Hartt wrote to the Secretary of the Edinburgh Committee for Dr. Cheever. He distinctly said in that letter sent in the winter of 1860, that I was to have so much on all the sums raised or obtained, and so the Secretary understood it.

But if Dr. Hartt and his Committee can afford to sustain the loss of public opinion, by this exposure in addition to other things not very pleasant in connection with this mission, I shall endeavor to sustain the loss of the money if it is not to be had without trouble. Perhaps Dr. Hartt and another member of that Committee mean to take this method of refunding themselves the hundred dollars which they gave between them to aid the mission.

However, there is one thing gained by this admission of the Committee in regard to the smallness of the amount as the proceeds of my agency, namely, that it affords another strong proof that the Church was not in the depressed financial condition as represented to me by Dr. Hartt; consequently the statement of Mr. Bennet, and the report of Mr. Berry, already alluded to, were correct, and that the Church was self-sustaining during those two financial years, whatever it may be now, and has not yet gone down.

E. JOHNSTONE.

In letter under date November 26th, 1859, Dr. Hartt informs me that the Church was then in a very harmonious state. His statement is as follows: "The Church is now in a more harmonious state than I have ever known it. All we require is money. We have thought it expedient to ask for $50,000; the interest of that sum would meet about one half the expenditure of the Church."

The Council then proceeded to hear testimony on the second charge, namely, the course of the Church in regard to the trial of Mr. Charles Abernethy, one of its members.

Mr. Abernethy said: The commencement of the discipline of the Church, was the receipt of the following letter from Dr. Cheever,

C. Abernethy, Esq.: New-York, April 14th, 1860.

Dear Sir: I regret to state that evidence has been submitted to me, and is before me, that you have charged me with manufacturing illegal and fraudulent votes during the election of Trustees, on the evening of March 12th.

You are also stated to have declared elsewhere, that it was your object and determination to remove me, or have me removed, from my office in the pulpit of the Church of the Puritans, and that you were confident this would be done within a short period.

From the slanderous and libelous portion of these declarations, I shall be compelled to seek immediate protection in law, unless you are disposed to retract and disavow the injurious representation.

But before any other procedure, it becomes my duty to seek an interview with you on the subject, and to state the injury that you have done me, that you may have ample opportunity to explain or disprove what you are said to have uttered, or, as a Christian man, to make such acknowledgment of the wrong, as is required by the Gospel.

From the prevalence of injurious reports, affirmed to have been put in circulation by your charges, and believed on your authority, any unnecessary delay is incompatible with what I owe to God, to the Church of which I am the Pastor, and to my own reputation in the world, which I am commanded by the Divine Word, to preserve unspotted as far as in me lies, for the sake of that usefulness which is imperiled by such a reproach as you are said to have cast upon me.

I am therefore compelled to request an immediate interview with you concerning this matter; and if it be possible for you to meet me this afternoon or evening, for the purpose of a kind and Christian conference in regard to it, I will be at my house for this purpose, or will meet you at yours, at any hour that you may find convenient.

I am truly yours,

George B. Cheever.

I sent this note in reply:

Rev. Dr. Cheever: New-York, April 14th, 1860.

Dear Sir: I found your note on my return home, and regret that my engagements are such that I can not see you this evening.

If convenient for you, I shall be happy to see you at my house, Monday evening, at eight o'clock.

Very truly yours,

Chas. Abernethy.

In accordance with this arrangement, he called on me at half-past seven o'clock, with Mr. Gilbert, a lawyer in the Church. He stated the charge which had been made against me, that I had accused him of manufacturing fraudulent votes, at the election for

Trustees. I told him that the charge was untrue, and I had nothing to say to it, but that. I could not own a charge which I considered false. He asked if I would deny it in writing. I said I would, if he would give it to me in writing. He found he had not brought it with him, and went home for it, and gave it me in his own handwriting as follows:

Mr. C. Abernethy charged Dr. Cheever, in our presence, with manufacturing illegal and fraudulent votes, at the annual meeting of the Society of the Church of the Puritans, March 12th, 1860. Upon being reminded by Dr. Hartt that this was a serious charge, and might lead to an action both before a civil and ecclesiastical court, he called in two witnesses, his partner, Mr. Collins, and a clerk, whose name we do not know, and said he charged that the votes which were cast upon Dr. Cheever's receipts were fraudulent and illegal.

(Signed) HENRY A. HARTT,
THOMAS J. HALL.

To which I afterwards replied as follows:

Dr. CHEEVER: NEW-YORK, April 27th, 1860.

DEAR SIR: The statement made to you by Dr. Hartt and Thomas J. Hall, of a conversation between them and myself, I do not regard as a fair and correct statement of the conversation.

Yours truly,
C. ABERNETHY.

The charge relates to a conversation at my store. Dr. Hartt had been there several times on business—I was a Trustee and the Treasurer of the Society at the time—and there were various business transactions connected with the Society going on between us. One day the conversation turned upon the subject of the recent election. I said that I considered certain votes that were cast, illegal. He said he did not. I replied that as we differ on that point, it is not worth while for us to discuss it, as the result will only be a wrangle between us; I shall not convince you, nor you me. The matter will be settled by legal adjudication.

Subsequently he came to my office, with Mr. Thomas J. Hall, who claims to have been one of the newly-elected Trustees. The conversation again turned on the subject of the election. I reiterated my conviction that the votes cast on certificates from Dr. Cheever for pew-rent, were illegal and fraudulent, and that they would be so considered by a court of justice. Dr. Hartt said to me: "You say that Dr. Cheever manufactured fraudulent and illegal votes?" I said: "You are putting words into my mouth which I did not use." I then called in my partner and book-keeper to hear the conversation. "I want what I say distinctly understood," I said, "so that when I hear of it again, if it should be misrepresented, I can contradict it." I then repeated in the presence of my partner and bookkeeper, what I had said before, that the votes cast on certificates from Dr. Cheever, I considered illegal and fraudulent.

Dr. Bacon.—The subject matter of the differences between Mr. Abernethy and Dr. Hartt and Mr. Hall, were certain votes that were given at an election of Trustees, Mr. Hall being one of the persons claiming to be elected, and Dr. Hartt another. The question of the validity of the election turned upon the validity of certain votes given by persons who brought Dr. Cheever's certificate that they had paid pew-rent during the year — a receipt signed by him that he had received pew-rent from them. And these receipts had been given on that very evening. The law requires a year's attendance and payment, to entitle a person to a vote. No money had been received by the Treasurer, (Mr. Abernethy.) These certificates were accepted, however, by the judges of the election as an evidence that the persons were qualified to vote.

Mr. Abernethy.—It was not usual for Dr. Cheever to receive the money in payment of pew-rent, and he had no authority for doing it; never but once or twice during my term of office did he receive any. The receipts were given on that evening, and no money had been paid on them or notice given to me. These receipts did not come into my hands, until fifteen or twenty days afterward.

But to return to the interview with Dr. Cheever and Mr Gilbert at my house. I told Dr. Cheever, the conversation between Dr. Hartt, Mr. Hall, and myself had not been fairly represented to him. He then spoke of the other charge against me—that I had stated that it was my object to have him removed from his place as pastor of the Church of the Puritans, and that I was confident that this would be done within a short period. I asked who told him this? He declined to say where he had got his information; but he said it was current talk. I said that I would not reply to a charge that had no better foundation, and I did not feel called upon to deny idle rumors. When he would show where his information came from, I would meet it. This he has never done.

A few evenings after this, I found waiting for me at my house, on my return home from business, Dr. Cheever, Mr. Hall, and Dr. Hartt. We passed a few compliments, and they said that they had called in reference to that subject again. I declined conversing upon it, as, after the misrepresentations that had been made, I did not feel safe. The next step was, that Dr. Cheever made a report to the Prudential Committee, giving statements that he called on me, and could not get any satisfaction, and wanted to know what to do. The Prudential Committee told him that they thought he had proceeded altogether wrong. His course, they said, was not according to the rules of church discipline as laid down in the Gospel, and they advised him to go back and do the thing over again. Dr. Cheever then came to see me again, and said he had come again on that unpleasant business. I still adhered to my statement, that the representations made of my conversation were not truthful, and I did not consider myself answerable for them. He said that I had done a great wrong, and that I was trying to raise a party against him in the Church. I told him I had raised no party against him; that he had made the party against himself. He said: "You ought to go away." I said: "I don't think so, Dr. Cheever. I think the time has come when you ought to go; and, I believe, if you would lay the case before twenty men of your own selection, they would agree with me." He said: "It's my pulpit." I said: "No, sir, it's not your pulpit." He said: "It *is* my pulpit." I said: "No, sir, the pulpit belongs to the Society." I said: "If I have raised a party againt Dr. Cheever, some body knows it. Bring forward any man whom I have influenced against Dr. Cheever." They never have done it. I have always been ready to answer any charges that they may be able to bring forward. I asked him to sit down and talk the matter over. He said he could not get any satisfaction from me, and left. The subject then went into the hands of the Prudential Committee. I do not know how it got into Mr. Gilbert's hands, but it was next taken up by him. About this time a new Prudential Committee came into office, containing some new members. Some idea of their action may be gathered from the following letter, which I received while in the country from Dea. Wm. H. Smith:

32 and 34 Vesey Street, New-York, 2d July, 1860.

Chas. Abernethy, Esq.:

My Dear Sir: I am sorry to annoy you while on a trip in a pleasant country; but think you will be interested to know how *our Church* gets on during your absence. Yesterday morning the Doctor asked the Committee to meet immediately after service, and I waited with others. The business before us was to hear the report of Gilbert and West, who, it seems, had been appointed to labor with you, to bring you, if possible, to repentance. I asked to have a report in writing. Was told it would be put in writing, but there had been no time to do it yet. I next inquired what particular sin or sins you had been guilty of? Was answered by Dr. Cheever, it was the sin of "schism." Then I asked if you were charged with any immorality, or any crime calculated to destroy your standing in the community as an upright, honest, and religious man? Answer: "No." "Do you then intend to exercise church discipline upon a man for a difference of opinion as to a course of policy, while you acknowledge his Christian character to be unimpeachable?" The Doctor answered, the law of Christ required that *schismatics* should be cut off, whether they were good Christians or not. It is the duty of the Church to do it for its own purity, and to secure the salvation of the schismatic. I ventured to express my dissent to this doctrine, and gave it as my opinion, that we all had the right to express our views as to questions of policy, and also that we might differ, not only among ourselves, but from the pastor, without being censured for it, or without injuring our standing as Christian men. The Doctor said in reply, we had no right to differ from him, and if we did, we had no right to utter our sentiments when at variance with those of the pastor. At this point Mr. Harvey said: "Then we may as well have a pope, and done with it; in fact, this is the essence of Popery." This brought the Doctor out in a grand oratorical display of indignant eloquence, and before the smoke cleared off Deacon Harvey went away; and I was left alone with the new Committee. It was then moved that a Church meeting be held to-night to take action in your case. I took the floor against this, and counseled moderation, and advised the Committee to consider well what they were doing, and proposed that the whole matter be postponed until the excitement of our late controversy had passed away; but I stood alone. *Drs.* Cheever and Hartt were earnest and violent for immediate action; and as it must be done before Cheever goes abroad, it must be done to-night, I then informed the Committee you were absent from the city, and would not be home, probably, in a week; which altered the appearance of things; and Gilbert and West were appointed a committee to inquire when you would be home; and then a *special* church meeting was noticed from the pulpit in the eve for Thursday eve, at which *very important* business *might* be brought. And so the matter stands. If you are here on Thursday, there will be an attempt made to discipline you; and the Committee seemed to be all in favor of such a measure, excepting Harvey and myself. Dr. Ball was absent. I don't know when you intend to be home, but suppose not till after Thursday. If you are not here, of course nothing will be done. I neither advise you to come or stay away. Come when you finish the visit you intended. The Church will do any thing the Doctor asks them to do, even to voting that our Church edifice is built of brick, and has two spires and only one sexton. The men that voted Thomas J. Hall into the Church will do any thing in the way of voting that men can do. The fact is, the whole establishment is getting to have a very bad flavor to me, and I wish I could get clear of such a concern, though at present it seems doubtful whether I can get away with even a character that would satisfy an Irish cook. I think we should make charges against Dr. Cheever, and have him tried before a Mutual Council, if he will, or before an *ex parte* if he will not go before a Mutual. The *interests*, if not the *reputation*, of Congregationalism require this at our hands. Let us do it.

In haste, yours, W. H. SMITH.

They appointed a Committee of Dr. West and Dr. Ball, to see me, which they did. I had nothing new to say, and I could say nothing more or less than deny the whole thing. Dr. Ball was anxious that I should go before the Committee, and I did so. I spent a whole evening with them, and the thing was talked over, and most of the Committee were satisfied with the explanation which I made. I may say, in fact, that all but two were satisfied; but those two seemed determined not to be reconciled. One of the Committee drew up a paper which embraced very much of what I had said, and wanted me to sign it. I asked them whether it would be satisfactory. They would not say. I said to them: "You know whether it will be satisfactory to you individually or not." They would not say. I said: "I do not want to put my name to any paper unless I know there is going to be some satisfactory end of the matter." A short time after that I received the following letter from Mr. Whiting:

Charles Abernethy, Esq.:

Sir: After it appeared that the first specification could probably be satisfactorily settled, and we passed to the second, I must say I was quite surprised to find you unwilling to say you had done wrong to the Church and pastor. It seems that your estimate of the rights of one opposed to the pastor is very different from that of the majority of the Prudential Committee, and, I suppose, from that of the Church. If this be so, still I think you could with consistency say to us, "My view has been, and yet is," so and so, "still I am willing so far to submit to the judgment of my brethren, as to pledge myself to remain under the decisions of the majority of the Church on all questions, or to take my letter and go to some other church. And I here concede that the majority of the Church of the Puritans has decided to retain Dr. Cheever as their pastor."

I write without consultation with any other members of the Church, but any thing you may wish to say, I shall be happy to show the members of the Prudential Committee. W. E. Whiting, 48 Beekman Street.

New-York, August 16th, 1860.

My only wish in this is to suggest a way of adjusting this difficulty, by which our Church may be saved the prolonged discussions we have had on other questions. May God grant us a large share of heavenly wisdom.

To which I sent the following reply:

Wm. E. Whiting, Esq.: Aug. 20th, 1860.

Dear Sir: I have received your note of the 16th. I made up my mind from the manifestations at the meeting Wednesday evening, that some of the brethren did not desire a reconciliation of the difficulties which they claim exist between myself and the Pastor of the Church.

I think my views, position, and acts have been misunderstood and misrepresented. Great pains have been taken to bring reproach upon me, and to prejudice the minds of the Church against me. Perhaps I am mistaken; I hope I am.

You may rest assured that no member of the Church has been more pained, and no one laments more the present unhappy condition of our Church than myself. I am ready to coöperate with the brethren in efforts to bring about a better state of affairs and feeling. If I am mistaken in my views of my rights, privileges, and duties, I desire to be put right. I do not wish to hold any improper views and opinions upon Church polity.

If during *all this trial* I have manifested an unkind, uncourteous, uncharitable, or unchristian spirit, I assure you I very much regret it, and desire the forgiveness of the Church and of its individual members.

(Signed) Yours truly, CHARLES ABERNETHY.

At the time this meeting was held Dr. Cheever had left the country.

DR. BALL'S STATEMENT.

Dr. BALL being called upon, said: There was at this time a rumor that our brother Abernethy was doing a very wicked thing in opposing Dr. Cheever, and in getting up a party opposed to him in the Church. I was among two or three others who took the ground that it was more than probable that our brother had been misrepresented; that he had stood up for Dr. Cheever in the former controversy, that he and his family had always been friends of Dr. Cheever, and that he had expressed great confidence that Dr. Cheever would be sustained, and that being somewhat discouraged with the ill-success of the anti-slavery ministry in the Church he might have let fall some remarks which had been too strictly judged. The Prudential Committee, of which I was a member, were called together by the Pastor, and he gave us a history of the matter, stating that he had been greatly tried by the course of brother Abernethy, and now more especially as the brother had brought a definite charge against him, involving his Christian character. He could not endure it any longer. He had proceeded at once to consult a lawyer in relation to the matter; he had written a letter to brother Abernethy, and then he took a lawyer with him and went and saw brother Abernethy, and got no satisfaction. He now wanted advice as to what was to be done. We were profoundly silent during the remarks of our Pastor, and I was led to speak first. I simply said: "Brother Cheever, as I understand the matter, we, as a committee, have nothing to do for the present. It seems to me, for one, that your steps have been altogether wrong; that you have omitted to take the first proper Gospel steps in settling a difficulty between yourself and one of the members of the Church. You must lay aside your lawyers and letters, and go to your Christian brother and meet him face to face."

I need not say that I uttered the sentiment of all the Committee.

They all agreed that our Pastor's course thus far was wrong, and only wrong. As one, I felt tried and grieved that such a course should have been taken, and yet it seemed to me that if he had testimony that this charge was really true, it was highly proper for him to investigate it. Dr. Cheever admitted that perhaps he had been hasty, or that he had not wisely gone about his work. It was then proposed by some of the brethren that perhaps the Doctor had better let the matter drop personally, and let some one of the brethren take it up, as aggrieved. Dr. Cheever went to see brother Abernethy, and reported that he could get no satisfaction, and brother Gilbert then agreed to take up the matter and prosecute against him. Brother Gilbert was requested to choose two of the brethren, and he chose Dr. West and myself, and we met brother Abernethy. For one I can say that I was so entirely satisfied from the interview, and from the history of the whole matter, that I thought this thing should be settled without going any further, and that the explanation made ought to be received. I urged the brethren of the Committee very strongly to come together and hear brother Abernethy's story, and I thought that would end the matter. I desired very much that the thing should be settled by the Committee, so that we might not have a Church trial, which I saw would be a protracted and difficult matter. I labored for this end. The Committee reluctantly consented to hold another meeting, at which the brother was before us. During the most of the meeting it really seemed as though the thing was settled. The Committee, with the exception of two, or possibly three, were entirely satisfied. These two or three charged that brother Abernethy was not honest in his explanation. According to the testimony of brother Hartt and brother Hall, they especially insisted that brother Abernethy did actually say that Dr. Cheever had manufactured fraudulent votes, and brother Hartt says that when he charged brother Abernethy that he was committing himself in the eye of the law, then he backed down, and made this explanation. Dr. Hartt justifies himself in reporting this to the pastor only, on the ground that he made an honest report. He says he did not intend to report this to the Pastor himself, but Mr. Hall did it, and after this he consented to give a written statement of the conversation as it occurred. When we charged Dr. Hartt that it was a very unjust thing when the brother explained himself, that he should go report it at all, that he should have let it die on the spot, he explained his conduct in this way,

QUESTION.—What reason did Dr. Cheever give for not being satisfied with this positive denial of the charge?

Dr. BALL.—The reason, as I understood, was that these two brethren are two witnesses, and that he is bound to believe them when they swear that the brother said that Dr. Cheever manufactured fraudulent votes.

Rev. Mr. ELLIOTT.—As I understand it, they declare that Mr. Abernethy said one thing before them, and another thing when his partner and book-keeper came in.

Mr. ABERNETHY.—In the conversation they accused me of saying a certain thing. I replied: "Dr. Hartt, I did not say so; I say so and so, and I want you to understand me," and I called two persons to hear it, so that if a report should come back misrepresenting what I had said, I could disprove it. They wronged me in reporting me to have said that which I distinctly disclaimed on the spot. I supposed that conversation would be the end of the matter. I did not think it possible that after using all these precautions I could be misrepresented.

Dr. BALL continued: As I said, it seemed for a time at this meeting of the Prudential Committee that the matter was settled, but it appeared at the end that two were not satisfied. They held that Mr. Abernethy had backed down from his first assertion because they had threatened him with the law.

QUESTION.—Were they dissatisfied then, that he had backed down?

Dr. BALL.—Yes, sir, that was their complaint, that he had said one thing to Dr. Hartt, and then backed out of it. I must say that Mr. Abernethy was a troublesome member to them, and if he would only have consented to go away they would have withdrawn the charges and given him a letter.

Rev. Dr. BUDINGTON.—This is it, then. Feeling that he was a troublesome member, they were not willing to let slip even a plausible ground of a charge against him, and so held on to it. His being troublesome was really the groundwork of this persistency in maintaining the charge. If I understand it, this was the real root of the difficulty; they wanted to get rid of him so earnestly that they had determined to make use of the first best occasion they had to accuse him, and they would not let the occasion go.

Mr. BENJAMIN K. PHELPS.—It was repeatedly stated by members of the Prudential Committee, that if Mr. Abernethy would take his letter and go away from the Church nothing would be done about the charges.

Mr. HARVEY said : On the first charge there was a vote taken, and I think only one, and that was Dr. Hartt, was dissatisfied with the explanation, provided the second could be explained. I do not remember whether Mr. Gilbert voted. In regard to the second charge, Mr. Abernethy would not consent unequivocally to pledge himself to support Dr. Cheever.

Mr. ABERNETHY.—I told them I could not pledge myself to support any man, because I did not know what he would do. My obligation was to support the Church.

Dr. BALL.—The result of that meeting was, that if brother Abernethy would take hold in the Church for Dr. Cheever, or take his letter, they would withdraw the charges. Dr. Hartt said to me frankly, when the recent effort was made to settle our difficulties, that this first charge he thought might be regarded as disposed of, and as to the second one, if the brother would only get up and say that if he had grieved any body, or done any thing that had offended any one, he regretted it, that the whole thing would be settled, and he would give a letter most cheerfully. I ought to say that one of the brethren who is now with the majority, said expressly : Brethren, if you are satisfied on the first charge, you are bound to be on the second, on the ground that it is too general to be entertained by any body. If these charges were brought against me, he said, I would pay no attention to them. This was the last action of the Prudential Committee. The Committee were through with it, and the matter appeared to be at rest, when Mr. Gilbert, the Clerk of the Church, brought the charge individually.

The charge by Mr. Gilbert was here read.

NEW-YORK, September 8th, 1860.

MR. CHARLES ABERNETHY :

DEAR SIR : My charges are as follows : That you have falsely accused Dr. Cheever of having manufactured fraudulent and illegal votes at the election for Trustees held at the Church of the Puritans, on the 12th day of March last, or words to that effect.

That you have for about a year past been engaged in a plan and effort to remove Dr. Cheever from his place, without any good and sufficient cause, and against the will of the Church, and that while he was engaged in a special labor demanding more than ordinary coöperation and sympathy on the part of his brethren in the Church, to awaken the churches of the land to a sense of their duty in reference to the sin of slavery. That in the carrying on and prosecution of this plan and effort, you have been guilty of the sin of covenant-breaking, and of disorderly conduct, and schism in exerting yourself, as a member and officer of the Church and Society, to divide the members of the Church and Society against the pastor, and against one another.

Yours truly, EDWARD GILBERT.

At the first meeting of the Church, for the purpose of hearing the charge, there had been no citation of Mr. Abernethy—he had not been notified. The meeting adjourned, and another was called for the 20th of September, of which Mr. Abernethy received the following notice:

NEW-YORK, September 18th, 1860.

MY DEAR SIR: On the 5th of September instant, at a meeting of the Prudential Committee of our Church, I was requested to read the charges against you which I had written, and of which you now have a copy. After hearing the charges, the Committee ordered me to forward a copy to you.

I wish also officially to notify you hereby, that I intend to present these charges at our church-meeting on Thursday evening the 20th instant.

Very respectfully,
EDWARD GILBERT,
Clerk of the Church of the Puritans.

CHARLES ABERNETHY, Esq.:

At this next meeting, after a long discussion, and after a statement by Mr. Abernethy to the Church, it was voted by a large majority, that Brother Gilbert be requested to withdraw his charges. The vote was carried immediately upon its being announced, and a great part of the persons present, supposing that was the end of the meeting were beginning to go, and a motion was made to adjourn, when a member of the Church introduced a resolution, that now all the members of the Church cordially unite in the support of Dr. Cheever as Pastor of the Church—a resolution of indorsement of Dr. Cheever's course, and pledging every body to sustain him. That resolution was put and carried, amid a good deal of confusion, in the midst of which the gas was turned out. Then a motion was made to reconsider the motion by which Mr. Gilbert was requested to withdraw the charges, and pending that reconsideration the meeting was adjourned to Monday, the 24th September.

Upon the adjourned day, the vote to reconsider was carried, and the Church voted to take up the charges against Mr. Abernethy, and in accordance with that, the following note was sent to Mr. Abernethy:

NEW-YORK, October 5th, 1860.

MY DEAR SIR: It is my duty as Clerk of the Church of the Puritans, to officially notify you that, on Monday evening, September 24th, the Church passed a resolution citing you to appear before them on Thursday evening, October 11th, and make answer to the charges preferred against you by me.

I have made ineffectual attempts to get hold of the minutes for a copy of the resolution, but have not been able to see Mr. Whipple.

You will please consider yourself officially notified hereby.

Yours in haste,

CHARLES ABERNETHY, Esq.: EDWARD GILBERT.

On the 11th of October, another meeting was held, when, after Mr. Abernethy had engaged counsel, and the trial had virtually commenced, the hearing of the case was adjourned for six months, to await, it was said, the return of Dr. Cheever, as his character might be involved in the testimony.

Mr. PHELPS.—Before the time to which the trial was adjourned, upon the presentation of a report by a committee with regard to a mutual Council—by a resolution which did not offer any reasons, which did not in the slightest degree refer to these previous charges, but was entirely foreign and distinct from them—Mr. Abernethy and five other members of the Church, by a naked resolution, were summarily suspended. This was a matter entirely distinct from the other. This suspension took place on the 22d of March, several weeks before the time to which the trial was adjourned, and at the time fixed for the trial, no meeting was called, nor held, nor has Mr. Abernethy had an opportunity to answer the charges against him to this day. At the time of the adjournment of the trial for six months, Mr. Abernethy entered the following protest against that action:

PROTEST OF MR. CHARLES ABERNETHY TO THE CHURCH OF THE PURITANS.

The subscriber, member of the Church of the Puritans, enters upon its records his solemn protest against the resolution passed Oct. 18th, 1860, by which the trial of the charges preferred against him by brother Edward Gilbert was adjourned to the second Thursday of April, 1861, and also against the refusal of the Church to permit the trial to be open and public for the following reasons:

It is an injury and a wrong to deny him a speedy trial. The unnecessary delay of any trial is an injury and a wrong to an accused person, who is conscious of innocence; especially to one who is assailed with odious charges on frivolous pretexts, which charges his accusers will not allow him the opportunity to disprove. This is the condition of the subscriber. He is assailed with odious charges. In the words of the complaint, he is charged, first with having "falsely accused Dr. Cheever," and second, with having "been guilty of the sin of covenant-breaking, and of disorderly conduct and schism."

The pretexts are frivolous. The first charge rests on a remark which he is alleged to have made concerning the conduct of Dr. Cheever, in giving receipts for pew-rents, in order to qualify voters for the election of Trustees of the Society. The second charge is founded on views expressed by him when a member and

President of the Board of Trustees, in respect to the financial condition of the Society, and the expediency of retaining Dr. Cheever as Pastor. In other words, his name is coupled with gross offenses deserving admonition, and if not confessed, deserving exclusion from the Church, simply for having exercised the right of "free thought" and of "free speech" in relation to matters which properly came under his cognizance, as President and member of the Board of Trustees. These charges were fully discussed in several meetings of the Church, and the trial of them was ordered to begin on the 11th instant, at which time the subscriber was cited by the Clerk to appear and answer: he did so appear, and claimed from his brethren the privilege and the right of an open and an immediate trial, that he might vindicate his innocence to the Church and his fellow-men, and expose the wrong-doing of those who have been active in originating this prosecution.

By the delay of this trial, without good and sufficient reasons, he is now subjected to the continuance of the reproach and suspicion which are involved in this formal arraignment, which has been so long in preparation. From this reproach and suspicion, he has asked to be relieved, in the only possible way, by confronting his accusers and their witnesses face to face, before his brethren sitting in open court, with the order and solemnity which become a Christian tribunal. By the denial of this reasonable request, he is deprived of the only privilege which is left to an accused person, which is not only his Christian right, but which is accorded to the meanest criminal by all civil tribunals under every free government.

2. The reason given for the delay of this trial is neither good nor sufficient. It is very probable that it might have been a very good reason why the action should not be brought, and the trial should not be ordered; but it is no reason at all why it should be delayed. The reason given is: "That it has been discovered that the accused intends to put Dr. Cheever on trial." To this he replies, that whatever ground of action he may have against the brethren of the Church who have done him wrong, or against Dr. Cheever, he would prefer before presenting such action, to have been first himself acquitted of the offenses with which he is charged. In managing his own defense, he can not bring Dr. Cheever to trial. If in the course of the testimony proper to this defense, it shall appear that facts unfavorable to Dr. Cheever are incidentally elicited, this surely will not be the fault of the accused, and will be no more than might happen in any similar trial; should such facts appear, it would be the duty of the Church at once to prefer charges against the Pastor before a proper tribunal. Such trial they should indeed delay till his return to this country, but after that return, to no remote period, especially if he should demand to be tried immediately. If there are facts of the kind suggested which must be exposed by the trial of the accused, for these facts and their publication the accused is in no wise responsible. To the hazard of having these facts exposed, Dr. Cheever has voluntarily subjected his own character, by allowing and enjoining this trial to be prosecuted in his absence. To this hazard and liability the accuser and the Church have also subjected the Pastor, by ordering the trial against the remonstrance of a large minority. But these hazards to the Pastor and complainant, however serious and formidable they may be, are incidental to the prosecution of this matter; meanwhile the object of their complaint is subject to the direct inconvenience, annoyance, and suspicion which arise from a definite and grave accusation. Is it right, or manly, or Christian, that the accused shall be forced to endure this annoyance for six months longer, in order that his accusers

or the Pastor should be relieved from the hazards of a trial which they voluntarily assumed?

3. There is an obvious and an easy method of securing relief to both parties — to the one from the incidental hazard which they deprecate; to the other from the direct wrong against which he remonstrates. The charges can be withdrawn. Such withdrawal would be ordered by any civil tribunal under analogous circumstances.

4. The honor of this Church requires that this trial should not be deferred. By such delay against the remonstrances of the accused and his friends, the good name of this Church will be brought into question, its reputation for fair and manly dealing will be dishonored beyond the possibility of recovery, the capacity of an excited majority to accord to a minority the measure of common justice, will be denied by those who judge us from without, and the possibility that in this enlightened city, and in the nineteenth century, a Christian church should govern itself, or discipline its members with success, after the methods which, according to the New Testament, were practiced in the first century, will be more extensively questioned than ever. Congregationalism, so honored in New-England by its successful workings, will be dishonored and disgraced in New-York by our example. Nay, the very Church which has claimed to be so conspicuous for its boldness and its zeal for the rights of the oppressed, will destroy forever its power to plead against injustice without, by this crying act of injustice within. Those who pass by our beautiful edifice, instead of paying it the homage of their respect as the fortress of that freedom with which Christ makes free, shall point at it, and say: "O liberty! what crimes have not been committed in thy name!"

In view of these considerations, the undersigned solemnly protests against the injustice and persecution to which he has been subjected by this act of the Church, and appeals to his Master in heaven.

In the name of that Master he renews the demand as his Christian right, that he may have a speedy and public trial, and the opportunity to vindicate himself before his Christian brethren and the Christian community from these unjust and injurious charges.

Charles Abernethy.

New-York, October 18th.

AFTERNOON SESSION.

The Admission of Mr. T. J. Hall to Membership.

The Council, not deeming it essential to take especial testimony in reference to the course of the Church in disregarding their rules and by-laws, as all the facts necessary might be expected to come out incidentally in the course of evidence, proceeded to listen to statements in reference to the course of the Church in the admission of Mr. Thomas J. Hall to membership.

Mr. White's Statement.

Dr. George H. White's statement of facts connected with the assumed admission of T. J. Hall to the Church of the Puritans, as presented to Council.

Mr. Hall had been a member of the Broadway Tabernacle Church some twelve years, more or less. He commenced attendance at the Church of the Puritans some three years prior to the spring of 1860, and was a member of the Society during a part or all of this period.

He applied for and received a letter of dismission from the Tabernacle Church and recommendation to the Church of the Puritans, said letter bearing date February 9th, 1860. The next regular season of communion of the Church was on the second Sabbath in March. Mr. Hall did not present his letter for admission previous to this communion.

On the evening of the 12th of March an election was held for three Trustees of the Society, Mr. Hall being one of the candidates of the party claiming, *par excellence*, to be the friends of Dr. Cheever. Deacons Wm. H. Smith and George H. White were, according to the Statute and By-Laws, appointed judges of the election.

The *apparent* result of the election was the choice of Mr. Hall and those associated with him on the same ticket. Subsequently, however, the judges gave certificates of election to Messrs. Harvey and Tompkins. Within a very few days, Messrs. Smith and White were called upon to answer in the Courts to a complaint made against them by T. J. Hall and two others, which contained this allegation, among others, that, notwithstanding all this, the said defendants George H. White and William H. Smith, and each of them, WRONGFULLY AND CORRUPTLY, DESIGNING AND INTENDING TO EVADE THE LAW, AND ALSO CONSPIRING TOGETHER TO INJURE AND ANNOY THE PLAINTIFFS, AND DEFRAUD THEM OF THEIR RIGHTS AND PRIVILEGES AS TRUSTEES, DULY ELECTED OF THE SAID SOCIETY, DID ILLEGALLY AND FRAUDULENTLY, AND TO THE GREAT TROUBLE AND DAMAGE OF THE PLAINTIFFS, give and grant to the said defendants Harvey and Tompkins certificates..

This complaint was made upon oath as follows:

City and County of New-York, ss.:

Henry A. Hartt, Thomas J. Hall, and William E. Whiting, all of said city and county, being by me duly and severally sworn, do each depose and say: That they are the plaintiffs in the above-entitled action; *that they have read the above com-*

plaint ; that the allegations contained therein are true of their own knowledge, except as to the matters therein stated to be on their information and belief, and as to those matters they believe it to be true.

HENRY A. HARTT,
THOMAS J. HALL,
WILLIAM E. WHITING.

Sworn to before me, this 30th day of March, 1860.

HERBERT BAILEY, *Commissioner of Deeds.*

This complaint bears date March 30th, 1860. The time for the next regular communion season was the second Sabbath in May following, the standing rule of the Church with reference to the communion and the admission of members being as follows:

Rule Eighth. The Lord's Supper will be celebrated on the second Sabbath in January, March, May, July, September, and November.

Applicants for admission to membership, either by letter or on profession, approved by the Prudential Committee, shall be propounded to the Church and congregation from the pulpit two weeks preceding the communion. They shall become members by election at the preparatory lecture ; and those admitted by profession shall, etc.

According to this rule, the last Sabbath in April was the time for propounding the names of applicants, and Friday evening, the 11th of May, the time for voting upon the admission of members previous to the May communion.

On Friday evening, April 27th, a prayer-meeting took the place of the weekly lecture, at the close of which the Prudential Committee met, according to previous notice, for the purpose of receiving applications for admission to the Church. No persons presenting themselves, the Committee adjourned. Before the members of the Committee had all left the lecture-room, it was announced that the letter of an applicant was in the room, and those who had not yet retired were requested to come together. Having met in response to this informal call, it was found that Mr. T. J. Hall was the applicant. There being but a bare quorum of the Committee present, it was suggested to defer action until there should be a fuller meeting. This was agreed to. It was found, upon inquiry, on the next Sabbath morning that the pastor was intending to propound Mr. Hall. This, however, was deferred, and the Committee were requested to meet at the close of that morning's service. This meeting was quite full, ten of the twelve members being present. Objections were made to the admission of Mr. Hall at *that communion.* Among others two brethren objected particularly on account of the allegation above quoted, which Mr. Hall had sworn to as true of his own knowledge.

They took the ground that this made a very serious difficulty between Mr. Hall and themselves. That it should be settled outside of the Church. That the Church ought not to become involved in it. That, to accomplish such a settlement, some time was requisite. It was urged that, inasmuch as Mr. Hall had attended the Church for nearly three years before obtaining his letter of dismissal from the Tabernacle Church, and after having obtained it, had voluntarily passed one communion without presenting it, it could not be considered as a hardship if his case was deferred for a brief period. The motion was made to propound Mr. Hall. This was lost. A motion was then made to postpone the case until the first Tuesday evening after the next communion. This was carried, three only voting in the negative. These questions were discussed with much earnestness and warmth for nearly an hour.

In this discussion, the pastor on one side took the ground that, if Mr. Hall's case was laid over by the Prudential Committee, as proposed, he might feel it to be his duty to bring it immediately before the Church, and have the question decided there, whether the Committee could thus usurp authority and keep an applicant for admission out. On the other hand, his admission at that time was very strongly opposed, brethren insisting that under the circumstances it would be a hasty disposition of the case.

At the evening service of this Sabbath, the pastor gave notice of a meeting of the Prudential Committee, to be held the next Tuesday evening, half an hour previous to the prayer-meeting. At the time appointed, the Committee met, but, instead of adjourning in time for the prayer-meeting, its session was prolonged until near ten o'clock. At the opening of the meeting, ten members being present, the pastor announced the business to be, the consideration of Mr. Hall's case—and this notwithstanding the Committee had, by so large a vote, decided to hold it under advisement until after the next communion. The subject was discussed at this meeting with much warmth and determination on both sides. The pastor and one other urging very strongly the necessity and obligation of admitting Mr. Hall immediately, taking the ground that the Committee had no right thus to oppose the admission of one coming without reproach from a sister church, and that if the Committee should adhere to their former vote, the proper course would be for the Church to take the matter in hand at once, and act independently of the Committee. On the other hand it was argued that the Committee had already disposed of the question until the specified time for its consideration should arrive. This haste, it was claimed, was both unreasonable and unaccountable. Mr. Hall had attended the ministrations of the Gospel in this house for nearly three years before he applied for his letter from another church. After obtaining it, he kept it in his own possession over one communion without presenting. If he chose to take this course, no one had a right to complain provided all else was correct. But it was claimed that, inasmuch as between the time of his obtaining his letter from the Tabernacle Church, and the time of his presenting it for our acceptance, Mr. Hall had done what some brethren declared to be a grievous wrong towards them; therefore it was not only clearly their right to have suitable time and opportunity to have the difficulty settled before Mr. Hall's admission, but also that this was the *only Gospel method.*

After much earnest controversy, the matter was left at the close of the evening where it was found at the opening of the meeting. That is, no vote of *any sort* was had, but there was a tacit consent of all present that the vote of the Committee on the Sabbath previous, laying it over until after the next communion, should govern.

On the next Friday evening a prayer-meeting again occupied the place of the regular lecture. At the close of the meeting Rev. Mr. Warren announced that there was an item of business to be attended to, and proceeded to present the case of Mr. Hall, and moved (in substance) that the pastor be requested to propound the name of Mr. Hall for admission to the Church at its next communion. Immediately a warm discussion ensued. All the members of the Prudential Committee who were present, with one exception, had voted for postponement in the Committee. They were very much grieved and hurt to find that the matter was brought forward in such a manner. The rules governing the action of the Committee, its rights and duties, and also the right of the Church and individuals in it to disregard the Committee, were somewhat discussed, until at length the motion for propounding was withdrawn and the meeting adjourned.

On the next Sabbath the Prudential Committee was called together at the close of the morning service. Several applications for admission to the Church were presented and acted on in due course. When these were finished, says the pastor: "Now, had we not better take up the case of Mr. Hall and dispose of that?"

This caused a renewal of the discussion, which had already been characterized by much acrimony and bitterness of feeling. The consideration of the matter at this time, however, was comparatively brief, as it was very soon made manifest that the minds of the Committee remained unchanged.

In the evening of this Sabbath, a call, signed by upwards of thirty members of the Church, was read, for a meeting of the Church, to be held on the next Wednesday evening. No business was mentioned in the call.

On Wednesday evening the Church came together, according to appointment. Mr. Fairbank was chosen Moderator. The meeting being opened, it was announced that the business before the meeting was the consideration of the case of Mr. T. J. Hall. A resolution was presented by Rev. C. J. Warren, the purport of which was, that the pastor be requested to propound Mr. Hall on the next Sabbath for admission to this Church. The discussion which followed was conducted in a very earnest, and for the most part, courteous manner. The meeting lasted till three o'clock the following morning.

The resolution was advocated by Dr. Cheever, Messrs. C. J. Warren, Hartt, Berry, and others.

It was opposed by Messrs. Smith, Ball, Bennet, White, Phelps, Chester, and others.

The attempt was made to show that the Prudential Committee, by their action in the case, were "like the Pharisees" of old, "shutting the kingdom of heaven against men, neither entering in themselves, nor suffering those were entering to go in." That it was done for the purpose of keeping the number of the pastor's friends small. This last charge was declared at the time to be a calumny, and the retraction of it was demanded, but none was made. The "dear brethren" were very affectionately appealed to to take Mr. Hall to their protection and embrace, inasmuch as he had recently give evidence that his mind was very tender on the subject of religion, and it was really very doubtful how it would go with him if the door of the Church should now be closed against him. It was also claimed that Mr. Hall was in the same category with two others in respect to the allegation and oath above referred to, and, therefore, the best way to manage the whole matter would be to have him also *in* the Church with them.

It was, moreover, a usurpation on the part of the Committee for them thus to lay the case over for one communion season.

On the other hand it was contended that so grave a difficulty as was involved in the allegation and oath on the one side, and the denial of the truth of that allegation on the other, was sufficient reason, by itself, why the Committee should take suitable time to have the matter settled. It was declared to be the real desire and purpose of the parties aggrieved to secure such settlement. It was shown, further, that Mr. Hall could not be propounded unless by a two thirds vote without violating the rules of the Church.

On the Friday evening previous to the communion, as it was postponed, the Church met for business purposes, to pass upon those members that were propounded. In the mean time, twenty-two members of the Church had signed a protest against the admission of Mr. Hall. The fact was generally known that the protest was drawn up and signed, and would be presented at the time when action should be called for upon this case. At this meeting, which was held in the lecture-room, the names of others who had been propounded were acted on. The pastor was standing over the desk with his head bent and his eyes upon the paper, and Dr. Ball was sitting at his right, only a short distance from him. In reading the names and taking votes, the pastor came to the name of Mr. Hall, and, in a hurried manner said: "Mr. T. J. Hall; those in favor of Mr. Hall say ay, those opposed, nay." At the moment that Mr. Hall's name was announced, Dr. Ball, who was to present the protest, stood and said in clear voice: "My Pastor, my Pastor." He spoke loudly and plainly, so that he was heard at the back part of the room. Dr. Cheever, however, paid no attention to him. For the time being he insisted that he did not hear him, although afterwards he admitted that he heard some sort of a noise. Objection was immediately made to the manner of the admission, as there were several who desired to speak on the question whether he should be admitted, and according to the rules of our Church every motion brought before it is open to discussion. Several of us rose to our feet and denied that the individual had been properly admitted. The Moderator (Dr. Cheever) peremptorily decided that he was a member of the Church, and there the matter was ended, as far as the action of the majority could put it at rest. During the course of the meeting the protest was finally brought in, edgeways, presented and permitted to go on file.

Dr. Bouton.—On the putting of the question in reference to the admission, did the pastor declare it a vote?

Mr. White.—Yes, sir.

Dr. Bouton.—But really there was no deliberate vote at all—there was no opportunity to vote?

Dr. White.—There was no lapse of time between the reading of the name and the calling of the vote, and the affirmative and negative votes were called almost together, so that there was a confusion of the ayes and nays, and no distinct vote at all. I should say that I, myself, rose to my feet with brother Ball, and called "Mr. Moderator" immediately on the announcement of the name, because I desired to express my views as to the propriety of church action in the case. It was considered very wrong to admit Mr. Hall while serious difficulties were pending between him and members of the Church, and without the action of the Prudential Committee.

Dr. Ball.—I was so impressed with the absolute certainty that the pastor heard me, that I insisted on knowing from him after wards, whether it was not so, and he finally admitted that he did partially hear me.

Mr. Chester.—I was in the back-part of the room, and I heard Dr. Ball. He called twice, and was heard all through the room.

Tests of Admission to Membership.

In regard to the fifth complaint in reference to the course of the Prudential Committee and the Church in establishing new, and as was believed, unscriptural tests of membership, Mr. Chester said he believed that it would not be necessary to bring forward any cases in addition to that related by Mr. Hunt as to the admission of Mrs. Harvey.

Mr. Hunt's Statement.

Mr. Seth B. Hunt said, since the Church by a bare majority indorsed the British Aid Mission it has held to its action. Indeed, the pledge to sustain this mission has been made a test of membership. The daughter-in-law of Deacon Harvey of the Church—his son is also a member of the Church—brought a letter from a Presbyterian Church in New-York State, recommending her as a suitable person to join the Church of the Puritans. It was taken in charge by the Examining Committee. I was not present at their meeting, but the facts were adduced at the next church meeting by inquiry. It appeared that at the lady's examination this Committee did not examine her as to whether she was orthodox in her faith, or was leading the life of a Christian, or whether she was a suitable person to belong to the Church, but the questions put to her were of another nature entirely. They inquired whether she was in favor of the British Mission. She said she was a stranger, and did not like to commit herself to any measure that she did not understand before coming into the Church. They said to her plainly that if she would not support this mission they would not present her name to the Church. As these facts were developed, I brought in a resolution of inquiry, and this whole testimony came out, and it was acknowledged by the party supporting the British Mission that they would admit no person to the Church who was not in favor of the British Mission. They said that this was an anti-slavery Church, and must be supported by British aid, and it was settled that persons becoming members must agree with it.

Mr. Harvey said in behalf of his daughter-in-law, that her examination was definite and positive in relation to her adherence to the British Mission and Dr. Cheever, and it was definitely laid down that no person would be allowed to become a member who was not sound on these points.

Church Committee's Report on Tests, adopted March 22d, 1861.

To the matter of the tests your Committee replied, that as the son of one of the leaders of the opposition had openly threatened that he was then going to work to do all in his power to bring in members to vote down Dr. Cheever's friends, that the Prudential Committee were justified, when his wife applied soon after for admission to our Church, in going behind her letter, and inquiring as to her state of feeling towards the pastor and the Church as then constituted. And that generally these tests were, under the circumstances, justified in order to prevent the threatened imposition of packing the Church with members hostile to us, for the purpose of voting out the pastor.

In regard to the complaint as to the course of the Church in regard to its internal affairs, and towards the Congregational body, its ministers and churches, general statements were made that it was frequently said in the Church that they did not care a straw for Congregationalism; and the respect shown for other churches of the denomination was seen in the manner in which they had refused to recognize this Council. Extracts were also read from the report of the Committee of the majority appointed to bring about a settlement of the difficulties of the Church, and presented at the meeting at which six members were suspended.

Extract from the Report of a Committee, adopted by the

Church March 22d, 1861, in answer to the request of seventy-six members for a Mutual Council.

Your Committee regard this as an aggressive measure, *designed* and adapted to obstruct the effort for an adjustment which has been strenuously made among ourselves. As a piece of strategy, it seems to contemplate the probability of the removal of many of the causes of disaffection, provided your Committee is allowed to prosecute its labors, and the consequent diminution and depletion of the strength of the opposition party. In the opinion of your Committee, the *object* of the movement is to bring discredit and odium upon the Church, by opening the flood-gates of the scandal of the press upon us in the rehearsal of our troubles, and the deliberations of a grave council upon them. The council would also afford opportunity for some not over-modest persons to expatiate upon their grievances, the purity of their record, and the lustre of their antecedents. Your Committee, for themselves, have no desire to enter upon such a farcical experiment. They are fully impressed with the conviction that no difficulties exist which we are not competent and adequate to adjust; and your Committee considers that it is with an ill grace that the opposition, after having created the state of things which alone justifies the British Mission and the institution of the protective policy in the matter of tests of membership, and after having done all in their power to prejudice against us the minds of those whom they would invoke to sit in council to judge us, should now propose an exterior tribunal before which the Church of the Puritans should appear as one party, and a factious minority, most of whom hold pews in and are attending other churches at this time, as the other.* Our motto has been, "Self-preservation is the first law of nature," and the Church has merely aimed to protect itself. The necessity of self-preservation has presented certain cases of disability under our Church constitution. In these cases, as in the British Mission, and in the tests, we have followed the course which in our judgment seemed authorized by the word of God. We have always been ready when these complaining brethren would remove the necessity for these *irregular steps*, to retrace the irregularity and annihilate the precedent. But so long as this opposition is prosecuted, so long by the soundest law and the best authorities, we are bound to protect ourselves, and, *if our Constitution and Church rules fail us*, we will fall back on the word of God. And we will not go into a Council. As well might the United States agree to arbitrate before a third power all her difficulties with the recreant State of South-Carolina.

The seventh question was not considered by the Council.

In reference to the complaint of the summary suspension of Messrs. E. W. Chester, Charles Abernethy, C. R. Harvey, George H. White, Thomas Rigney, and Joel Blackmer, who were among the applicants for a Mutual Council, without any form of charges or complaint being made, or any notice or intimation of trial.

A report of the meeting at which this action was taken, from the *N. Y. Daily World*, was read; also report of Committee in reply to the request for a Mutual Council.

---

* Some six persons had taken pews, and about twenty-six have thus sought edification elsewhere. More than this number sympathize with us, who did not have opportunity to sign the call. —*Note by Committee.*

Extract from the Report of the Church Committee, respecting suspension from membership, adopted March 22d, 1861:

Your Committee are constrained to note here another case of seeming disability under our Church Constitution, arising out of this factious and persistent opposition of several leading members of this Church to its pastor, its welfare, and *by inference* to the blessed cause, which, through and by means of the Church, we seek to promote. Our Church Constitution provides for discipline, only in case of private offenses, where one brother has cause of complaint against another—in which case the rule in Matthew is to be followed. Offenses of a schismatical or disorderly nature, although in a certain sense private, are in their main features public offenses. *Specific charges and* PROOFS *are superfluous* in such cases. The Scripture makes it incumbent on us to withdraw from such as walk disorderly, and after a Church has borne long with brethren thus disposed, and labored with and for them until the burden has became vexatious and intolerable, and especially until the influence of the Church is in danger of being impaired by longer submitting to their unnatural and enforced fellowship, there can not be a doubt but it then becomes the duty of the Church to deliberately suspend them from the rights and privileges of membership, which they hold *only to abuse.*

Mr. WHITE.—I did not know that there was any complaint against me, or that any action of the Church was proposed. I was not present at that meeting, and to this day I have never received the slightest intimation from any body in that Church that any such action has been had in my case. They have never notified me that I am suspended from the Church.

Mr. CHESTER said that the Committee of the complainants had now presented to the Council all that was supposed necessary to give a full knowledge of the facts in reference to these complaints. Before leaving themselves in the hands of the Council, the complainants would say that they had nothing to ask for themselves personally. They would consent to any disposition of themselves which would be best for the interests of the Congregational body.

Dr. BACON said that the question now arose with the complainants, whether they were to connect themselves with other churches; or were to consider themselves as bound by the covenant which had heretofore bound them to each other, and which they maintain that the majority has broken and departed from, and so be recognized as a church to maintain the ordinances of the Gospel by themselves. He supposed they were willing to be advised on these points, and would probably accept any advice that the Council might give.

Some cursory remarks were then made by several of the complainants in reference to their future action.

Dr. BACON then spoke as follows:

I do not propose, Mr. Moderator, to go into another rehearsal of the facts which have been submitted to the Council, nor to recapitulate at all the various specifications which are before you in printed form, and which have been before you while you have been hearing all the testimony. I suppose that the mind of every member of the Council is already made up as to the substantial and essential accuracy or otherwise of each general allegation of matters of fact, and of each specification or item which is given in the printed form. I therefore propose nothing more than to call the attention of the Council to what I suppose to be some important principles of Church order, and, indeed, of Christianity, which are involved in this case, and upon which the Council, I think, is called to pronounce an opinion.

I begin with this point: *the method of supporting public worship in our churches, and the rights of ecclesiastical societies.* Our system recognizes a distinction between the *church*, strictly so called, and the *ecclesiastical society* or parish. The one is the spiritual body, including only the communicants; the other is a civil corporation, including or intended to include, the whole body of habitual worshipers. I may be allowed to assume that the members of a worshiping assembly have rights. I do not mean all the hearers that may be present on a particular occasion, but the stated worshipers, whether they are communicants at the Lord's table or not. They have rights that are guaranteed to them by the law under which these ecclesiastical societies are incorporated. And it is an essential principle in American Congregationalism, or, at least, in New-England Congregationalism, that it recognizes and guards all the proper rights of the stated worshipers in a parish. It recognizes the existence of a parish, as well as of the spiritual body of communicants in the parish. It makes its distinction broad between the secularities of the worshiping assembly and the spiritual interests of those who are bound together by the Church covenant. The house of worship is built as the Lord's house by the ecclesiastical society;—the civil contract is made between that corporation and the chosen minister, who is not chosen by the election of the church exclusively, but is their own choice as well. Nothing is better settled in all the usages, practices, and principles of our Congregational churches than this — that the minister is not to be imposed upon the parish without the free choice of the majority; and the legal right of the voters of the parish to complain of the minister, and to appeal for protection against any maladministration on his part, is recognized continually. It has been a theory, I know, with some of our brethren at the West, that it would be much better to have no civil corporation other than the church. I believe that was the theory on which one church in Boston acted for a while,—that the church should own the building and whatever property there might be; make the civil contract with the minister; give the orders for shingling the roof, or any such business. But the experience of a few years convinced that church that their way was unwise; and now the same system exists there as in all the other parishes of Massachusetts; the rights of the church being guarded on the one hand, and the rights of the worshiping assembly — of every man recognized as belonging to it — acknowledged on the other:—the right of the church to keep its own communion pure, to see that pure doctrine is taught in the pulpit, and to regulate all matters relating to the spiritual concerns; and the right of the corporation to regulate all matters relating to the secularities of the concern.

The present troubles in the Church of the Puritans began with a difficulty in regard to the temporal affairs of the *Society*. It was thought that the support of the pastor was growing precarious. Whose business was that? In some sense it was the business of the Church. But it did not belong to a few members of the Church to take out of the hands of the ecclesiastical Society a business of that nature,—the providing of ways and means for the support of public worship. Yet it was in that error that this British Aid enterprise began; it being assumed by those who undertook it, that the Society, and the trustees elected by them according to law, were going to neglect their duty, or were incompetent to perform their duty; and on that assumption this mission was instituted. If it had been a mission to raise funds that should be placed in the hands of the proper authorities, the constituted agents of the congregation, there might have been no harm in it. But the plan of it, as you have seen, was a plan to usurp, by a self-constituted committee, the proper functions of the Society and the Board of Trustees; and to obtain a power to control them. That undertaking, in the very beginning of it, was a virtual violation of good faith on the part of those commencing it—a conspiracy against the congregation and the Board of Trustees.

But there is another aspect of that scheme, which deserves distinct attention. It is sometimes objected by those who do not understand the workings of Congregationalism, called "the voluntary system," that it makes the clergy dependent on their hearers, and is a temptation, therefore, to the clergy to be unfaithful to their hearers, and to preach only what the congregation like to hear. The answer to that is—and it is a very conclusive answer—that there is no where to be found an established church, a church which makes the ministers the beneficiaries of the state, and independent of the people to whom they minister—there is no where to be found any church in any Christian land where, in point of fact, there is so much of fidelity, so much of independence on the part of the ministry, so much of boldness in maintaining what they consider to be true, as there is among the ministers who are dependent entirely on this voluntary system. And the reason of it is, that wherever there is a Christian people, with the Bible in their families, with the Sabbath in their sanctuary and in their dwellings, the people like faithful preaching and faithful ministration, and will not be contented without it. And that connection between ministers and their hearers is proved by facts to be more effectual in securing fidelity and usefulness on the part of the clergy than any other relation. Now this British Aid scheme turns out to be a scheme for making Dr. Cheever independent of his hearers, and dependent on something else—dependent on a certain number of trustees to be originally appointed by himself, and with power of filling up their own vacancies. For that reason, I think this undertaking to send an agent abroad for the purpose of raising an endowment of $50,000 was in violation of good faith towards the Society, and in violation of a principle which ought to regulate the action of the Church.

There is still another view to be taken of this whole affair. That edifice was built by men who put their money into it on certain conditions, expressed or implied; their idea was that they were building a church—a house for the worship of God according to those forms and those principles which were familiar to them, and which we call Congregationalism. They had confidence when they formed the Church and the ecclesiastical Society connected with it, that the working of it was to be in conformity with certain principles, forms, and usages. It was on that understanding that they invested their money; and they did not give their money absolutely, but took title-deeds to pews. I do not think that is the best way of building churches, but still it was the way adopted here, and is the usual way of building houses of worship in New-York. They had rights then in the building, and they never consented that a majority of the communicants in that Church, still less that the person who might be pastor of that Church, should own and control the property; they expected that the property would continue to be at the disposal of the ecclesiastical society under the legitimate influences of the preaching of the Gospel, and of a church organization conducted according to the order of the Gospel. What have they got now? Their property is gone—they might as well have invested it in Virginia State bonds; it is not worth as much to-day as the bonds of that seceded State—or Mississippi repudiated bonds. There has been an unfair game played with them. The whole history of these proceedings down to the present hour has been an attempt—we might almost say a willful attempt—to destroy the value of that property. It is destroyed. If it had been covered over with lava from Vesuvius it would not have been more fatally destroyed.

In this connection I want to speak next of *the sin of schism.* I believe that the brethren for whom I speak were represented as guilty of the sin of schism—a schismatic and factious minority. It is worth while then to think, and, if we can, think clearly, of what constitutes schism in a church. There is such a thing mentioned in our translation of the Bible. The word is Greek, and comes from a root which signifies to tear, to rend. It is not a difference of opinion between members of a church, that makes schism; and, indeed, schism does not lie in opinions; nor is a difference of opinion between the pastor and this or that individual in the church a schism. The right of free opinion and thought implies diversity of thought; and no diversity of thought among those who hold to the truth as it is in Jesus, and who agree in accepting Christ as their Master and their Guide, and his word as their rule—no diversity of opinion among those who thus agree—constitutes schism. A difference of opinion about the site of a meeting-house is not a schism. If forty-nine are in favor of having it built in one place and forty-seven in another, that is not a schism; so of questions of policy. A difference of opinion about particular measures—public measures—a difference of opinion whether to give to the American Board of Foreign Missions or to the American Missionary Association is not a schism. A difference of opinion about a minister, whether he is the best man or not in the place, whether he is too old or young—that is not schism. All these things are unavoidable, and are a part of the liberty which belongs to the members of a church. Members must have leave to consult with one another; they must have the amplest liberty to consider—and therefore to meet that they may compare and digest their opinions. They have a right to meet together and agree what they will do; they have the right to act together. This, therefore, is not schism; it is the democracy of the Church.

So long as all parties expect the majority to govern, and are willing that the majority should govern within the legitimate sphere of church action, so long there is no rending of the church—no schism. An essential thing in the government of a church is the democratic principle that the majority is to govern—the constitutional majority, in all questions included within its constitutional powers. That is essential to the being of a democracy, and therefore to the being of a church. I say, the majority is to govern within the legitimate sphere of church action. I wish this to be borne in mind, that when the majority in a church undertakes to govern in matters that do not belong to a church, then the person or persons aggrieved need not submit. The thing done must be a thing which the majority have a right to do. To use a power that shall control or defeat the majority acting in the sphere of church action, is schism, or leads to schism inevitably. For example, if a minority say, "We will not submit to the vote of the majority," on a question over which the church has jurisdiction, they are guilty of schism. If they undertake to depart from the church, or if they undertake to make the church uncomfortable to the majority in any way whatever, when the majority has clearly and fairly pronounced itself on a question on which the majority has a right to decide, then that minority is guilty of schism, whether they go out of the church or stay in it. Now here is the case of this British Aid Mission. I think the members of the Council are convinced that, upon the showing of the man who projected it, who loveth to have the preëminence in this matter, and to whom that preëminence belongs—I do not mean Dr. Cheever—it was undertaken for the very purpose of taking the power out of the hands of the majority. It has been justified on the ground that majorities were unsafe and fluctuating, and majorities were open to conviction—might change their minds—and he wanted to have a fund of $50,000 by which he could control the majority and overrule them. That was schism in its beginning, and the present majority, in carrying out the policy thus inaugurated have become partakers in the sin. I think that will become more and more manifest the more we think of it.

I come now to speak of *the standing rules of a church.* One of the complaints relates to the violation of the standing rules of the Church by the majority. The standing rules of any church, so far as they are any thing else than a statement of Christ's law—for *these* standing rules are simply, in some of the most important things, nothing else than a statement of Christ's law, for instance, the one which is merely a repetition of Christ's law as recorded in the 18th chapter of Matthew—I say, the standing rules so far as they are any thing else than a statement of Christ's law, are in the nature of a compact between the church and its individual members, concerning the way in which the legitimate business of the church shall be prosecuted under the law of Christ. The church has no right to make any standing rule that is any thing else than that. For if the commination which stands at the end of the Apocalypse against him that addeth any thing to that book, is true of the Bible as a whole, it is certainly true against those, whoever they may be, that undertake to add any thing to the law of Christ for the government of his Church. I should rather take the responsibility, awful as it would be, of adding to the revelation which the Gospel gives us of eternity, than undertake to add to the law which Christ the Master has given in the Scriptures. No church has a right to add one jot or tittle to the law of Christ, in the shape of standing rules; and so far as the rules of any church are any thing else than a repetition and summary of the law of Christ, they are, as I have said, of the nature of a contract between that church and the individual members concerning the way in which the business of the church shall be transacted under the law of Christ. Such are the rules of this Church about the mode in which business shall be transacted, about the way in which a church meeting shall be called, about the mode in which persons shall be examined for admission to the Church. All these are not additions to the law of Christ, nor modifications of it; but they are notices given, in which the Church pledges itself to the individual members of the Church that the business is to be prosecuted in this particular way. None of these rules, therefore, can be laid aside in an irregular way by an arbitrary act of sovereignty without involving in the act of sovereignty a sovereign breach of good faith towards the individual members of the Church. And where they are arbitrarily set aside, as they have been in this case, all disorder is the necessary result, as has happened here. You remember what was said last night in regard to the setting aside of rules. They wanted to disfranchise a certain portion of the members of the Church, so that the majority would be with them; and so, finding that they could not actually alter the rules of the Church, they altered them by imposing upon one particular rule an interpretation of their own, foisting upon it a meaning that had never been in it, and never could be there by any legitimate principle of interpretation. And again and again rules have been overridden—trampled on at the convenience of this factious majority—for a majority can be factious as well as a minority.

We come to another point: *What is the nature and proper function of a church?* The question is before this Council, whether this majority are the Church? I think it is a great question. I commend it to the serious and candid attention of the Council whether they are the Church. The fact that they have prayer-meetings does not make them a church. There are legislative prayer-meetings sometimes—there are prayer-meetings in a penitentiary sometimes. The fact that there are preaching does not make them a church. The fact that the building they meet in has a steeple or two steeples, as the case may be, does not make them a church. A church, I believe we all hold, is a body of Christ's disciples, joined to each other by a covenant to walk together as Christ's disciples, for their mutual edification, and for the administration of the law which Christ has given to such societies.

Let me read here the definition of a church, as given by the venerable Synod at Cambridge in 1648. Having affirmed that "the state of the members of the militant visible church, walking in order," is, "since the coming of Christ, only congregational," and "therefore neither national, provincial, nor classical"—in other words, that schemes of national, provincial, and classical church government, are, since the coming of Christ, without warrant,—the Synod proceeds to say,

"A congregational church is, by the institution of Christ, a part of the militant visible church, consisting of a company of saints by calling, united into one body by a holy covenant, for the public worship of God, and the mutual edification of one another in the fellowship of the Lord Jesus."—*Camb. Platf.* c. ii. § 6.

This passage is from the chapter on "the *nature* of the Catholic church in general, and in special of a particular visible church." In the next chapter, the Synod proceeds to describe "the matter" or material, "of the visible church," in these words:

The matter of a visible church are saints by calling.

By saints by calling we understand, 1. Such as have not only attained the knowledge of the principles of religion, and are free from gross and open scandals, but also do, together with the profession of their faith and repentance, walk in blameless obedience to the word, so as that in charitable discretion they may be accounted saints by calling, though perhaps some of them be unsound and hypocrites inwardly. . . . . 2. The children of such, who are also holy.—C. iii. §§ 1, 2.

The meaning of this phrase "saints by calling," and with it the idea of what a church is, receive a further illustration in the chapter "of the admission of members into the church."

The weakest measure of faith is to be accepted in those that desire to be admitted into the church; because weak Christians, if sincere, have the substance of that faith, repentance and holiness, which is required in church-members; and such have most need of the ordinances for their confirmation and growth in grace. . . . Such charity and tenderness is to be used, as the weakest Christian, if sincere, may not be excluded nor discouraged.—C. xii. § 3.

I wish to call the attention of the Council to this. The material of which a church is composed, is the disciples of Christ—those who make a credible profession of discipleship. They are those whose faith is visible—a matter that can be taken cognizance of. The church does not profess to include those whose faith is not visible, but only those whose faith can be seen and recognized. The last extract that I read implies what I want the members of this Council to take notice of; it implies that there is no right on the part of the Church to shut its door against any one of Christ's disciples—no right to require of candidates for admission to its communion any thing but this, that they are Christ's visible disciples, giving credible evidence of belonging to him, and of desiring to walk according to his doctrine and in obedience to his precepts. No church has a right to add any thing to that in its conditions of membership. It has been said that our churches do require more than this. Perhaps they do; but if they do, I apprehend it is a result which time has wrought, making a difference between the principles on which they were originally established, and the position to which they have drifted unthinkingly. It may be said that some of our churches, at least, refuse to admit members who are not sound, in their estimation, on certain disputed doctrines that are not held by all Evangelical Christians;—that our churches, for example, are Calvinistic, and that their professions of faith are intended to exclude Methodists. I believe that in point of fact our churches do not exclude men whom they regard as Christian men, even though there may be some doubt in their minds on some questions of a particular doctrine. I believe that often when a candidate has intellectual difficulties on such points of doctrine, the church consents to waive them. We have learned to admit that men may be comprehended in the Divine decree of election who do not believe in the decree of election at all, as defined in books of theology. And the principles of Congregationalism require our churches to say, as most of them do say in effect, that we receive to our holy covenant all who give us evidence that they belong to Christ.

The bearing of all this on the matter before the Council is not hard to be discovered. Here is a church which has undertaken to be something else besides a church — a church which has long ago adopted the principle that it was to be constituted by selecting out of Christ's disciples a particular class. It undertakes to be a class-church. The test of membership has come to be something like this: "Do you believe in Dr. Cheever? We do not want any body here unless he gives satisfactory evidence of fealty and loyalty to Dr. Cheever." It is not pure Christianity, but Cheeveranity, that they go for. Such an institution is not a church. It has lost sight of the proper functions of a church, the proper duties of church members and church officers, and all for which a church has a right to exist in the name of Christ. They have a building there on Union Square, what they call a citadel; I am glad to see the flag of the Union over it, but I doubt very much whether it is a church. I want to know if a church has a right to say: "We are not going to have any black men in this church"? Have they a right to say, "No body shall belong to this church who wears a beard," or "No body shall belong to the church who has not studied Algebra"? Have they a right to say, "This is an anti-slavery church, and no body shall belong to it who does not pronounce our shibboleth on the subject of slavery"? Have they a right to say to a man, "You are a good Christian enough, but you are not one of our stamp; you had better go to Dr. Thompson's or Dr. Spring's church; we do not want you here"? I say no. Have they a right to say, "This church is going to be a tract society, with a printing office, and a book-binding establishment, and we are going to carry on this business: —tract societies sometimes invade the province of the churches; we will take up the functions of a tract society, and carry on the business of making tracts"? Why may they not say, "This church is going to carry on an India-rubber manufactory, and if any body will not invest in the stock, he shall not belong to this Church"? I use these illustrations for the sake of making it perfectly plain that a church has no right to exist for any other purpose than for that of being a church of the Lord Jesus Christ, and has no more right to supplement or add any thing to the constitution of a Christian church as it is laid down in the New Testament, than it has to bind up a book of its pastor's sermons with the Testament of our Lord Jesus Christ, as a book of authentic scripture.

In proof that the views which I am presenting are not strained, I may read here one sentence which I find quoted from the preface (by the Editor in old England) to Davenport's treatise on "the Power of Congregational Churches."

> There are two things which run through this whole discourse, and are legible in every line of it: First, that the power of churches is confined to their *res propria*, their own proper matters; second, that there is not any spiritual church power, to which they are by the institution of Christ subjected:—two grand and pillar principles of the Congregational Way.—*Congregational Dictionary*, Boston, 1852; p. 66.

I need not say to this Council that John Davenport was not only, as some one has called him, "*Puritanorum Puritanissimus*," but an Independent of the Independents; nor that he studied such questions with an accuracy and thoroughness not surpassed by any other of the New-England fathers. Those two "principles of the Congregational Way" which run through his treatise on "the Power of Congregational Churches," run also, more or less distinctly, through the web of every other argument on that side of the church-question in that age. "Pillar principles" indeed they are. The first was no less important in the controversies of that age than the second. The many superstitions which Romanism had engrafted on the simplicity of Christian worship, attempting to make them obligatory, and which the national church of England had so imperfectly reformed, fell before the first and were broken; while the liberty of individuals to associate in churches, without asking leave of any ecumenical or national organization, rested on the second. The first of these pillar principles is not only historically related to the second, but is logically essential to it. The independence of the church is its dependence on the authority of Christ. Because it is Christ's Church, its proceedings must be conformed to the charter which he has given it; and its power—the democratic power of its majority—is confined to its *res propria*.

To put the same thing in another form of statement, we are not to understand that a Congregational church may be a church and something else. It was not the idea of our fathers when they wrought out this system, that a Congregational church is to be distinguished from other churches by certain specific qualities additional to the generic character of a church; it was merely that a Congregational church is a church and nothing else. It was the idea of a church "pure and simple." A Methodist church is a church and something more; it is distinguished from other churches by its positive institutions. And so of all those bodies which have the idea of a national or sectarian church. But a Congregational church is a local church, a distinct body of Christian believers, associated in conformity with the teachings of Christ; and nothing else. That is the whole idea of a Congregational church; it is a church and nothing else. The idea upon which they have proceeded at Union Square, from the beginning of these troubles, has been that they were to be something else than a church; and that is where all the trouble has come from. There are no legitimate tests of membership additional to credible profession of faith in Christ. No one who is, in the language of the old Cambridge Platform, a saint by calling, is to be excluded when he desires, in conformity with his duty, to become a member. In Union Square they have adopted a contrary principle.

The next point to be considered is the question of *fellowship with that majority of the Church of the Puritans.* I regard that majority as having abdicated the charter of a Christian church, and as no more governed by New Testament rules of church order than a political meeting in Tammany Hall. It has forfeited its church character by trampling on all church principles and rules. I say this in no unkindness to Dr. Cheever, with whom I have none other than friendly relations, and who, not being before this council, is not to be held responsible for the acts of that majority. But I have no hesitation in saying that the majority, by their whole course, in relation to these brethren, have lost their right to a place among our churches.

The subject of the communion of churches one with another, is one which the Council will of course consider, and include in their result. The chapter in the Cambridge Platform, from which I quote on this subject is, I think, one of the most exact, logical, and fortunate in its forms of statement, of all in the whole Platform. I will read from that 15th chapter entitled, "Of the communion of churches one with another."

The communion of churches is exercised sundry ways. 1. By way of mutual care, in taking thought for one another's welfare. 2. By way of consultation one with another, when we have occasion to require the judgment and counsel of other churches, touching any person or cause wherewith they may be better acquainted than ourselves. . . . . But if a church be rent with divisions among themselves, or lie under any open scandal, and yet refuse to consult with other churches, for healing or removing of the same, it is matter of just offense both to the Lord Jesus and to other churches, as bewraying too much want of mercy and faithfulness not to seek to bind up the breaches and wounds of the church and brethren; and therefore the state of such a church calleth aloud upon other churches to exercise a fuller act of brotherly communion, to wit, by way of admonition. 3. A third way then of communion of churches is by way of admonition. . . . . As one apostle might admonish another, so may one church admonish another, and yet without usurpation. In which case, if the church that lieth under offense do not hearken to the church that doth admonish her, the church is to acquaint other neighbor churches with that offense which the offending church still lieth under, together with the neglect of their brotherly admonition given unto them; whereupon those other churches are to join them in seconding the admonition formerly given; and if still the offending church continue in obstinacy and impenitency, they may forbear communion with them, and are to proceed to make use of a synod or council of neighbor churches walking orderly (if a greater can not conveniently be had) for their conviction. If they hear not the synod, the synod having declared them to be obstinate, particular churches approving and accepting the judgment of the synod are to declare the sentence of non-communion respectively concerning them; and thereupon, out of religious care to keep their own communion pure, they may justly withdraw themselves from participation with them at the Lord's table, and from such other acts of holy communion as the communion of churches doth otherwise allow and require. — *Camb. Platf.* cxv. § 2.

There are details of proceeding here which are not authoritative—nothing about the book is authoritative except what is reasonable. It is the *rationale* that has force, and not the detail. I submit that the method to be observed in the withdrawal of communion from a church, is that which has been observed thus far in the present case, namely, for the party aggrieved, as this minority has been aggrieved, by the scandalous conduct of this Church, by the opprobrium that it has brought not only upon the name of Congregationalism, but upon the far more sacred name of Christ, to call together such a representative body as this, and submit the whole case to such a body, and take their advice on the question whether the churches walking in the order of the Gospel should not, henceforth, withhold from that Church, all acts of communion. That is complying, I apprehend, entirely with the spirit of the rule laid down by the Cambridge Synod more than two hundred years ago.

The question then comes before this body: The churches have sent you in reply to the call of this minority; they have sent you to look into this matter in their behalf. You have no authority over the Church of the Puritans; you can not reverse their action; you can not send a writ ordering them to correct their records in any respect; you have no control over that property; — but you have a right, in behalf of the churches that have sent you, to say whether or not that Church has departed from the divinely-appointed order of the Church of Christ — to say whether or not the condition of that Church in respect to discipline and order, is a scandal to the name of the Church and to the name of Christ. And if it is your judgment that such is the fact, then you have the right to advise the churches which you represent, and all other churches walking in the faith and order of the Gospel, to withhold communion from this factious majority, and henceforth to interchange with the Church of the Puritans no acts of the fellowship of churches. That sentence will not, of course, take effect by the mere authority of this Council — it will have no effect except as it is accepted and adopted by the churches to whom it may go. It is nothing but a recommendation to the churches. It is no usurpation of authority. Your published result — supposing it to be such as I have described—will be a notification to the churches that a council — such a council as this—a council called from the remote parts of the country as well as from the neighborhood—a Council called for the especial purpose of bringing together men who were under no suspicion of complicity with the sin of pro-slavery — has found this Church to have departed from the faith and order of the Gospel, and from the duty of standing for the faith as it is in Jesus. It is an advice to the churches to take notice of the facts. Then when the question comes up, "Will you sit on a council to which the Church of the Puritans is invited?" that involves the question, whether you will recognize the Church of the Puritans as a church in fellowship with you. If a person bringing a letter of dismission from the Church of the Puritans comes to any church, the question comes up: "Will you receive this person on the certificate of commendation from the Church of the Puritans?" And if this advice is given and followed, they will refuse to receive him on that certificate. Or the question may be: "Will you dismiss a member of your church to the Church of the Puritans?" If this advice is given and followed, they will refuse to dismiss to the Church of the Puritans. The churches will refuse to interchange any of the customary acts of the fellowship of the churches with that Church, so long as it continues to walk in this disorderly manner. And if the rule to withdraw from a brother that walks disorderly is followed, how much more should the rule be followed in its application to a church walking disorderly. That is, as I conceive, the whole meaning of the withdrawing of fellowship from a church.

Mr. Elliott said, he supposed that this withdrawal of fellowship from the Church would affect the Pastor only in his relation to the Church; it would not affect our relations to him ministerially, except as in his specific connection with the Church.

Dr. Bacon continued: These seventy-six brethren and sisters who have appealed to this Council, also submit the question whether the aggrieved members and such as may unite with them, shall not be constituted and recognized as a church of the Lord Jesus Christ, in the Congregational order, in place of the Church of the Puritans, if they should so ask of the Council. I suppose that the question was set down with a very imperfect comprehension on the part of the aggrieved as to what they might desire to do in the circumstances—without a very definite desire on their part, as to whether it would be best for them to continue to be a distinct church by themselves, or to merge themselves, by dispersion into other churches. I will only say a word or two in regard to the position in which they stand to one another to-day. They are members of the Church of the Puritans, or were, when it was a church and was not any thing else. They entered into covenant with one another individually, and with all the rest of that church, to walk together in mutual love and brotherly helpfulness according to the law of Christ, as a worshiping body—a body of disciples, associated for maintaining public worship, and for each other's edification, and in that way for the advancement of Christ's kingdom. That covenant holds them to each other now. It is not dissolved by the violation of it on the part of the majority. The union of these States is not dissolved by the secession of one State, or seven States, or seventy-seven States; the Constitution stands as long as there are three States remaining to hold together under it. If they choose to hold together under it, the secession of one after another — the violation of it by one after another, does not annihilate the Constitution. Just so, in this case: here is their covenant, which is their covenant with Christ, and with the whole fellowship of Christ's redeemed on earth. That covenant does not cease to bind them to one another in consequence of the violation of the spirit and essence of the covenant on the part of the majority in that Church. And now, if they are disposed to say, "We will not abandon in despair the enterprise upon which we entered some fifteen years ago; we will still pursue that enterprise; we love one another, and we desire to walk together as a Christian church, and we hope that soon better times will come, and that then we shall be able to obtain a house of worship and have a minister settled, and all the ordinances of Christ maintained; we consider ourselves bound to each other still; we will worship together; for the present we will go to some other church, till this present calamity in our national affairs be passed, and then, as soon as it is overpast, we will proceed with our enterprise"—will this Council advise them to take such a course? Will this Council recognize them as a church of Christ? If this Council will say, "We recognize you as a church from whom the majority has departed, and we will give you the right hand of fellowship, and we invite you to go on and hold up, here in this great metropolis, the standard of our Christian faith"—if you thus advise them to go on, and if they are willing to go on, I submit that there is no need of their calling another council, for the purpose of putting them through the motions of forming a new covenant and adopting new rules. There is the profession of faith that they have already made; there is a covenant that binds them to one another; there are the rules which they have adopted and consented to, and which the other party has trampled down and violated. Why should they not be recognized as a complete church? For the present they may be obliged to unite with some other congregation before they can get a house of worship. I have suggested these views in regard to the nature of a church-covenant, for the sake of bringing that matter in the same distinct way in which it lies in my own mind, before the minds of the Council.

There is a very important and practical lesson to be learned, not only by ministers, but by all Christians, by all church-members, from the catastrophe that has fallen upon that enterprise, which a few years ago was so full of hope—the Church of the Puritans on Union Square. I have nothing to say—I desire most carefully to avoid saying any thing that shall imply any censure of the Pastor of that church. I do not think that the present troubles are so much to be ascribed to him as to another man, a man whom I do not know personally. In the progress of these revelations, as vial after vial has been poured out, I have thought of this passage in the third epistle of John: "I wrote unto the Church, but Diotrephes, who loveth to have the preëminence among them, receiveth us not. Wherefore, if I come, I will remember his deeds which he doeth, prating against us with malicious words; and not content therewith, neither doth he himself receive the brethren, and forbiddeth them that would, and casteth them out of the Church."

I presume he cast them out without a trial. I have said nothing of that very extraordinary proceeding. I do not think that I could say any thing which would add to the impression which the simple narrative of it, as presented here in the documents, produced upon the minds of the Council. When these brethren in good, regular standing, were turned out of the Church, or, as the phrase is, suspended, every principle of church government was violated. The very phrase, "suspended," is an idiom foreign to the Congregational order. There are only two censures in the New Testament, and therefore only two in a Congregational church; one is *admonition*, which, as some of the old writers say, worketh suspension. The church puts a man upon trial; after the private dealing with him by individuals, the church inquires into the case. If it finds him guilty of the sin charged against him, it admonishes him. Even admonition, however, can not be administered, as a suspension was in this case, without telling a man what he is admonished of. Admonition, in the necessity of the case, implies that there is a charge, and that the church has found the man guilty in some way under that charge. Before proceeding to exclude any body from the Lord's table, the church must find him guilty of some act, and must find that act on his part to be a violation of some rule of the New Testament, or of some command of the Decalogue; and then their admonition—if the offender does not repent and bring forth fruits meet for repentance—prepares the way, in due time, for the other censure, which is the censure of *excommunication*. But in this church, or synagogue, or whatever it may be called, the whole system and theory of church discipline is trampled upon. Men, I was going to say, are found guilty without trial; but no, they are executed without being found guilty. The proceeding is more summary than a drum-head court-martial. A man is called up—no, without being called up, he is merely sentenced; with no trial, no preferment of a charge, no opportunity of defense, the man is cut off from the Church, and to this day never has received from the Church any notification of the fact whatever. This is the kind of proceedings which you are to consider, and on which you are to pronounce an opinion.

I leave the matter in the hands of the Council, thanking them for the patience with which they have heard us; and trusting that God will guide them to give such counsel to those who have called them, as will be for his own glory, for their edification, and for the good of the Church.

EVENING SESSION.

Each member of the Council was called on for his individual opinion in reference to the decision to be arrived at by the Council.

The calling of the roll was suspended, and the following members were appointed a Committee to prepare a report to be presented as the result of Council: Rev. Dr. Sturtevant, Judge Taylor, Rev. Mr. Gulliver, Rev. Dr. Budington, and Rev. Mr. Wolcott.

Dr. PALMER said: As I am under the necessity of returning home to-night, and must shortly leave the Council, if Dr. Bacon will allow the interruption of his remarks, I will give, in very few words, my views of the case before us.

The whole matter properly before the Council seems to me to resolve itself into two questions: First, Have these brethren who, without trial and opportunity for defense, have been summarily excommunicated, been fairly treated by the Church? Secondly, Ought this Council to recommend that the fellowship of the Congregational churches be withdrawn from the Church of the Puritans?

To the first question, I answer emphatically, NO! It is contrary to all justice, to every principle of common law and common-sense; it is an outrage upon religious liberty, and utterly subversive of the established rules of Congregational Church discipline, thus to cast men out of the Church without even a form of trial. It is equally at variance, in letter and in spirit, with the rule laid down by Christ himself for the treatment of a supposed offense, and with a true Christian temper. The act of the Church, so far as appears, admits of no justification. Nothing, indeed, can justify illegal and oppressive proceeding on the part of a church in the administration of discipline. It is my opinion, therefore, that these brethren are entitled to be set right as regards their Christian standing, so far as the opinion of this Council may avail; and that we ought either to give them letters of recommendation to other churches, or, if good reason appear, to recognize their right to be organized into a new church.

So much for the first question.

To the second, I answer without hesitation, YES. A Congregational church is one that, receiving the common faith of the great Puritan brotherhood, administers its government in accordance with the well-known principles of the Congregational Church polity. When any church sets at naught these principles, it ceases, *de facto*, to be a Congregational church. It becomes an alien body, having no longer any claim to the fellowship of the churches with which it was before united by common usages and sympathies. We have no control over the Church of the Puritans, and must leave it to act as it pleases. But we ought, I think, to say what is true in fact, that it has deliberately and wholly trodden under foot the principles of discipline which all our churches recognize, and should therefore be held as no more of us. I do not regard it as a Congregational church any more than I do the body that is accustomed to meet in Tammany Hall. I am not called upon to say that its members are not Christians. That is another question. But the Church on Union Square, I repeat, *has ceased by its own acts to be a Congregational church;* and I think it is our solemn though painful duty to say this to the churches to whom the polity of our fathers is still dear.

These, in brief, are the views which, as a member of this Council, I should wish to see embodied in its result.

Rev. A. L. Stone said: Mr. Moderator, I could have wished, as has been suggested, that some of the wise fathers on this Council had been first called upon to state their views of the case submitted to us; but I am willing briefly to utter my own impressions.

I do not purpose to go over the ground, one by one, of the charges and complaints against the Church in the paper of grievances put into our hands. I wish simply to say, in regard to these allegations, that so far as the evidence laid before us enables me to judge—and I am satisfied both with the fairness and comprehensiveness of that evidence—I am convinced that THE MAJORITY, calling themselves the Church of the Puritans, have violated and transcended the Christian idea of a church, the rights of the trustees of the parish and of the body of stated worshipers, the most sacred and precious rights of these appellants, and the principles of Congregational order, amity, and fellowship.

I do not review the evidence sustaining these conclusions in my mind, but I am irresistibly led to these conclusions. I therefore judge that majority deserving of the most emphatic and faithful rebuke which this Council can administer. We are not at liberty to withhold that censure; we are bound to utter it, for the sake of those brethren themselves, that they may be led to repentance; for the sake of the public scandal which the procedure of this Church has caused, that that scandal may be removed from our body; for the sake of the cause of anti-slavery, which has been wounded in the house of its friends; and for the sake of future histories, to open in this same scene, and to be enacted on this same theater.

Then, sir, I think it is our duty to sustain these appellants; to accord to them the rights of which they have been unjustly deprived; to restore them to a position of church-fellowship, and to secure to them the possibility, if they shall so desire, of a regular organization as a Christian church.

It will be for them to say whether they will be immediately constituted and organized by this Council as a church of Christ. For myself, I should not judge that step to be wise at the present time. If I were one of their number, the last thing I should covet would be a church organization under the name of the Church of the Puritans. I think that name is in evil odor. It is a stench in the nostrils of men. It would be, in my judgment, a curse and not a help to these brethren to start on any basis with such a title heralding their way to public confidence. They would have a long and hard battle to fight at the very outset, to redeem that name from the taint which pervades every syllable of it.

Nor do I suppose these appellants are quite ready to be constituted into a new church. Still, if they wish either of these courses, I believe it is *a right on their part* which we can not deny to them.

These points, sir, briefly indicate the results which I think our action ought to secure.

Rev. JOHN P. GULLIVER, of the Broadway Church, Norwich, Ct., said, that the course of the Church of the Puritans, in all their dealings with this minority, seemed to him neither Christian, judicious, manly, or wise. He had never read, heard, or imagined any thing like it. It was a difficult thing to know whether to laugh at it or be angry at it. It is such a tissue of absurdity and wrong, as he would not have thought possible of Tammany Hall. The interests of Congregationalism and the interests of the Christian Church had been ignored and forgotten, and another object exclusively had taken possession of these men's minds, which they seemed to have pursued with utter recklessness.

In the case of this British Mission, a contribution is asked in the name of the Church, but without the sanction of its officers, for the purpose of placing the control of the Church in the hands of a few individuals. The principle which makes the pastor dependent on the church is here violated.

The Council had no power to declare that the Church was not a member of the Congregational body, but it could recommend, for reasons given, that the Congregational churches withdraw their fellowship from this Church. The result of the Council would probably be published to the world ; this result should be drawn up with very great care, and should be made exceedingly clear. He would suggest that it commence with a statement of the facts in the case, selecting the strongest. The grounds of complaint should be brought out so that they could be read in a short space of time, and be understood with perfect distinctness. Then the principles upon which such facts should be dealt with should be stated, so that churches might see in what ways Congregationalism is capable of dealing with these difficulties.

He would recommend a withdrawal of fellowship from this Church, and that the severest penalty should be inflicted that was possible for this Council. The Church had scorned this Council, had scorned the Congregational churches, and had disregarded the request for a mutual council.

Mr. Theodore McCurdy, delegate from the same church, said he should advocate a withdrawal of fellowship from the Church of the Puritans. In regard to the future action of the complainants, he would recommend that the matter be left mostly to their judgment.

Rev. Dr. S. W. S. Dutton, of the North Congregational Church, New-Haven, Ct., said it was evident, from the testimony in reference to the British Aid Mission, that, to say the least, there had been a good deal of crookedness in that matter. Gross deception had certainly been practiced by some parties in the Church, and the Church should have dealt with them in the way of discipline. It appeared, however, that instead of this, the Church had afterward indorsed their action. He thought that the complainants had attached too much importance to the subject, although he was free to confess he considered it an unwise and injudicious action. It was certainly very unjust in a few individuals to put the Church before a foreign community in the attitude of beggars, and it was also a very serious wrong for them to collect funds, not for the Church, but to be placed in the hands of a power beyond the control of the Church, to carry out party purposes.

But he thought the proceedings in regard to the trial of Mr. Abernethy were more important; they were an outrage on all

Congregational practices of dealing with members; they were an outrage upon all equitable practices of dealing with any body before any tribunal; they were unworthy any body of men, much more of a Christian church.

In the case of the admission of Mr. Hall, wrong was done to the minority, and the matter was carried forward in violation of congregational rules, and of the rules of justice and common sense.

In regard to the establishment of new tests of membership, he considered it as serious an offense as a church could commit, to adopt rules and tests in violation of or in addition to Christ's rules. When a party in a church, in order to carry out the purposes of a party, adopt new and utterly unscriptural tests, there could be no more serious wrong.

If he had any stronger superlatives, he should use them in reference to the summary cutting off of six members of the Church, who were evidently of the highest Christian respectability, and fair and open in their mode of dealing, without trial and without charges. It was clearly the most violent sort of ecclesiastical lynch law. He never heard any thing like it.

When a church persistently refuses to regard the fellowship of the churches, and will not permit a council to be asked of sister churches, ignoring the churches in this respect and repudiating fellowship in that form—that, of itself, is sufficient ground why fellowship should be withdrawn from them. He was very clear that the Council should recommend the withdrawal of the fellowship of the Congregational churches from them. In all the forms in which fellowship is expressed, he should utterly deny it.

In reference to this minority, he considered that it was not necessary that they should be constituted anew, for they were already in covenant with Christ and in covenant with other churches.

Dea. Nathaniel Jocelyn, the delegate from the same church, said, that he should be sorry to see this Council take an instantaneous act of discipline against this Church. It would create an unpleasant and doubtful feeling in the minds of many Christians all over the country, who do not happen to be thoroughly posted up in the facts of the case. He hoped they would reïnstate and justify these complainants, and that whatever was done with regard to the other body, would be considered in the light of an admonition.

Dea. A. S. Kibbe, delegate from the Congregational Church, Albany, N. Y., said he had only heard the testimony since that in reference to the trial of Mr. Abernethy, but he confessed that from what he had heard, his opinions were widely changed from what they were before he came here. His impression had been that there was a faction in the Church who were opposed to the anti-slavery preaching of Dr. Cheever, and that the Church was divided into two parties—a pro-slavery and an anti-slavery party. Those opinions had been dissipated, and he found that the complaint was a course of wrong action on the part of the Church. He was willing to agree heartily in the Council condemning the course of the Church, and reïnstating these brethren who had been aggrieved.

Dea. HENRY W. TAYLOR, delegate from the Congregational Church, Canandaigua, N. Y., said there had not been a church in which he had felt so strong an interest as in this Church of the Puritans. But it turned out that this case did not depend on anti-slavery. He thought the Church had done wrong. He held to a liberty in Congregational churches which was to be exercised by the church. The British Mission was in violation of this principle. He believed the whole proceedings of the Church to be in violation of the doctrines and principles of the Congregational Church. But still, whatever judgment the Council arrived at was an *ex-parte* judgment, because the Church had not been heard in their own defense. They had been invited to come, it was true, and if they feel aggrieved by any action of the Council, they can call for a Council to settle the matter.

Rev. M. E. STRIEBY, of the Plymouth Church, Syracuse, N. Y., said his feelings and surroundings would lead him to sympathize very much with Dr. Cheever and the Church of the Puritans. He came to this city with a disposition to regard and keep before his mind the view of the majority of the Church, because of their high position on the question of slavery. But after hearing the testimony, mostly from documents emanating from the majority, he thought this British Aid Mission was badly conceived, and carried on in an improper way, and that the Church, by indorsing the whole proceeding, took it upon their shoulders, and precluded, as had been suggested, any trial in the case. With respect to the other doings of the Church, of which it was complained, he considered them in violation of all rules of congregational order and Christian privileges. With all respect for Dr. Cheever, he perceived that there might be a great difference between Dr. Cheever and anti-slavery. He was, therefore, prepared for a severe censure of the Church.

He thought the question as to what should be done with these complainants, was merely a prudential question, and should be left to them, to do what they should think best.

Mr. Ira H. Cobb, delegate from the same church, said, it was hard to pass upon a question in which only one side had been heard. He liked to look upon both sides of a case, especially one of such importance as this. The proceedings of the Church, as they appeared from the testimony, seemed very strange, but he was not prepared to indorse all that had been said in condemnation of them. He thought that the complainants should form a new church.

Rev. Samuel Wolcott, of the New-England Church, Chicago, Ill., said he was present at the installation of Dr. Cheever, and had felt a very great interest in his success.

He considered that the proceedings brought to the knowledge of this Council were very just matters of complaint. He thought that in the trial of Mr. Abernethy the rules of Congregational order were never more completely violated, from the letter threatening him with a lawsuit to his suspension on another ground, and the denial to him of a trial on the first charges. The whole proceeding, from the beginning to the end, was an outrage on Mr. Abernethy. The summary suspension of the six members was in the highest degree improper and disorderly, and in violation of every right which belonged to them. He thought the Council could not do less than to recommend the withdrawal of fellowship from this Church, at least until it gives some evidence of having receded from their unjust position. It may be that in time another class of men from those who now control it will take the lead in the church, so that it can come again into Christian fellowship.

These seventy-five or more complainants do not ask that the Council give them letters of recommendation to other churches; and they do not want the Church of the Puritans to receive them back again. The very last thing the Council could do would be to recommend them or any one else to that church. The speaker did not see what the Council could do except to recognize the fact that they had never forfeited their membership in that church. He thought the best way for them to do would be to remain a distinct body, and keep up their organization as a church.

Rev. Dr. Wm. I. Budington, of the Clinton Avenue Church, Brooklyn, said that when a few members in the Church of the Puritans attempted to raise a fund in support of the Pastor, they encroached upon the recognized right of the trustees. In the other proceedings brought before the Council, he considered that the complainants were sinned against.

By the refusal to recognize the last Council that was called, by their entire contempt for this Council, which is a mutual Council in its spirit, by the Church taking no notice of either, he regarded them as, by their own act, and by the silent and inevitable workings of common fame, out of the fellowship of the churches.

QUESTION.—Would you receive a member from that church ?

Dr. BUDINGTON replied, that he would not receive a member from that church unless he came with a confession of sin upon his lips.

The history and course of the Church of the Puritans had been quoted against Congregationalism often by those whose interests and prejudices would naturally lead them to make use of such arguments, whereas Congregationalism had stood a fair trial in this city, and, he maintained, had come out as unscathed, as he prophesied this Government would come out unscathed from the secession trial. He believed that, as the result of this Council, Congregationalism would be planted upon a higher platform and a more advanced position than it had ever been placed before. Congregationalism was to be shown in this community, as the result of this Council, to be a system which combined the strength of orderly government with fullness of individual liberty. He spoke of this more emphatically, because he should claim of these brethren who had given additional reason for confidence by the discreetness with which they had prosecuted this matter before this Council and in the late Church of the Puritans, that they should form a church by themselves. The Council should demand it of them that they stand by the old flag.

Rev. Dr. THOMPSON, of the Broadway Tabernacle Church, New-York City, said he had deep sorrow about this whole case, because of the personal associations which it involved. At the time of the establishment of the Church of the Puritans he had hailed the event with great joy. He had stood by Dr. Cheever in all his difficulties, until he found that he himself had been made the mouth-piece of a sham presentation, and was denounced in England as having no sympathy or interest in the anti-slavery movement. At the very time of the thousand dollar testimonial, when it was openly proclaimed here that the Church was out of debt, this mission of mendicancy to Great Britain was *secretly* planned, and men who here had stood by Dr. Cheever BECAUSE of anti-slavery, were slandered abroad as wanting in fidelity to that cause! The attempt was made to support Dr. Cheever at the expense of the good name of brethren who had preached and labored against slavery as long and as faithfully as himself, and who had stood up for him before this community. And yet to-day he stood by Dr. Cheever in the way of apology, explanation, and defense, so far as to almost alienate personal friends who were disposed to censure the pastor, as well as the majority, for these irregular and arbitrary proceedings of the Church of the Puritans. Nothing that Dr. Cheever had spoken or might hereafter speak against himself in these matters, could ever betray him (Dr. T.) into a harsh or unkind word toward Dr. Cheever. Having for fifteen years watched the growth of Congregationalism in this city, as a system favoring Christian liberty, human freedom and all true progress, he was grieved beyond expression at the scandal brought upon the principle of church independence and the cause of anti-slavery by these late proceedings of the Church of the Puritans. The British Aid Mission he considered radically wrong, because it was a scheme to deprive the Church, for years to come, of its appropriate, organic right and duty to look after the pulpit in its ministrations, and an attempt to set the pulpit above the Church, by investing the pastor himself with an independent money power which no minister should ever have in his hands. It was a radical subversion of the principles of church organization, which this Council could not countenance. A war in favor of liberty can not be carried on by setting up a despotism in the pulpit. The Church had trampled upon the most sacred rights of the minority, justifying itself by the supremacy of the will of the majority. But the Church is under a higher law of Christ, and has no right to violate that law by a majority vote. The speaker recommended that the result of the Council should contain an explicit statement of the reasons why the churches should not recognize an association that thus overrides every principle of Christ's law, as in fellowship with them as a Church of Christ. He was sorry for certain members of the Church of the Puritans, who, because of its many dear associations, did not desire to leave the Church, and yet did not fully sympathize with these disorderly proceedings. He strongly recommended that the complainants form a church by themselves instead of dispersing among other churches. Another vigorous Congregational church in New-York was much desired by himself and his own people.

The Council then adjourned until Saturday morning, at nine o'clock.

SATURDAY MORNING SESSION.

Dea. Austin Abbott, Delegate of the Broadway Tabernacle, said that the object of the conduct of the majority of the Church appeared to be to create a church membership, not for the progress of Christ's cause, but for the direct purpose of controlling church action. That was a wrong purpose, and means intrinsically wrong have been resorted to to carry it out. On the one hand, they have excluded from coming into the Church those who would oppose the policy sought to be carried out; and on the other hand, they have cast out of the Church those who, in the Church, opposed that policy. That is the explanation of the casting out of members, and of the establishment of tests of membership unknown to Congregationalism.

He was prepared to vote for the withdrawal of fellowship from this Church, and he did not see how any testimony could alter that result. These actions of the Church, he supposed, were undeniable, and they were attempted to be justified by the parties who had led the Church in this course, on the ground of a supposed necessity.

In reference to the question as to the advice to be given to these brethren, he felt that it would be entirely nugatory to advise the Church to receive them again. The Council might recommend these brethren to the fellowship of other churches, and authorize a committee to give them letters to other churches; but then there was another party in the case who had hardly been mentioned; there were the brethren who had called this Council; the majority of the Church who had taken a course against which the minority had protested; and, thirdly, there was a neutral party, there were absentees, there were some sick who had been concerned in these affairs. There were always members of a church in good and regular standing who were out of sight. The Council should care for these, and the only way to do this was by recommending these brethren to continue in their church relation. The Council should recognize the complainants as a church of Christ, in virtue of their present confession of faith and their present rules. If these brethren will hold to their organization, if they will, in the spirit of kindness, in the spirit of meekness which they have exhibited before the Council, receive any and all of the individuals who may come to them, and thus keep a door open for brethren in the Church who have taken no part in these unjust proceedings, then full justice might be done to all parties. For these reasons, the speaker was prepared to recommend that fellowship be withdrawn from the late Church of the Puritans, and to vote also to recognize these brethren, and such as may associate with them, as a Church of Christ in fellowship with the churches, by virtue of their present covenant and confession of faith.

Rev. H. B. ELLIOTT, of the Bedford Congregational Church Brooklyn, N. Y., said, in regard to most of the points which were covered in the specifications, he thought the complaints had been fully justified. It seemed to him that the first point was fundamental. The grievance was not in the fact that certain brethren chose to use their individual liberty in obtaining funds for the support of the pastor or of the church, as they might deem expedient; but that the manner in which they attempted it, and the object which they sought—to place an irresponsible body over the church in effect, or over the society — and the manner in which the whole thing was conducted, was such as to give these complainants, as Christian men as well as members of that association, grounds for deep indignation and grief; and that they could not have done less than they have done in publishing their position in this whole matter from the beginning. The course of the church in relation to the minority has been based upon the feeling that the agreement with this British Mission was a fundamental matter. He thought that the Council should justify the minority in their whole course as based upon their position in this first matter. In regard to the trial of Mr. Abernethy, the admission of Mr. Hall to membership, and the action of the Committee of the church, in establishing new tests of membership, there appeared to be but one mind; and it was not worth while to waste superlatives in reference to them, although, certainly, no language could be much too strong to express the disapproval, by the Council, of these proceedings.

The speaker had felt a good deal of hesitation as to the course to be adopted toward this church. Being commissioned as delegates and pastors of the various churches, it was to be presumed that they would accept the action of the Council, yet it was not absolutely sure that as majorities the churches would vote as the members here were prepared to vote, not having heard the full statement which had been presented here. He had no question but that the churches would sustain the Council fully in any vote of censure it might choose to pass; but whether they would consent to go so far as to unconditionally withdraw fellowship, so as not to receive a member with a letter from the Church of the Puritans, so as not to exchange pulpits with the pastor, so as not to assist in any council where that church might be called, was somewhat questionable. He should be glad to be sustained in such action; he believed the church fully deserved it — as fully as any church which had gone over to some fundamental heresy, or had committed itself to a vice flagrant in the sight of the world. He should be willing, therefore, to vote that each of the members, as representatives of the churches, take this case to the churches, with the recommendation of withdrawal of fellowship. He doubted that the Council could pronounce this sentence on the church as consummated here.

Dr. Bacon.—That is not proposed.

Mr. Elliott thought that the result of the Council, though it recommended the withdrawal of fellowship, should state that this is not done finally, and should contain the exception that if by some proper and accepted action a change should be manifested in this church, the fellowship of the churches should be restored to it. The fellowship should be withdrawn until, by some appropriate action, they manifest a change of character.

The speaker, in reference to the tenth point, felt difficulty on the point that had been made, that these brethren could regard themselves as a church, if they chose to do so, by virtue of the covenant into which they have entered with each other and with the Church of the Puritans; and that they could go forward, simply taking their by-laws, rules, confession of faith, etc., and appoint their officers, select their pastor, and proceed to do all provided for in the covenant of the Church. He thought that their covenant did not hold ecclesiastically when they ceased to be members of the Church of the Puritans, if that church remains as a church. When they go forth from the church their covenant is so far forfeited; the Church of the Puritans being to them no longer their church, their covenant ceases with each other as members of a church.

Rev. Mr. Wolcott.—If the majority had become Unitarian here, would you have recognized the minority as the true Church remaining?

Mr. Elliott said this was a hard question, still he should say that a majority in a church ceasing to retain their integrity as a Christian church, having become Unitarian, the minority might be recognized as the church. He did not see that the Church of the Puritans had lost its integrity. If the churches withdraw fellowship from it, on the ground of their disapproval of the course of the church, it still remains an orthodox Congregational church, and its identity as a Christian church remains. The Council could not say it was not a Christian church, but they could say that it had taken a most unchristian part. He was not prepared to say that it had ceased to be a church, as one that had become Unitarian, and he could not conceive that these brethren were the church, because there could not be two churches in one. The only regular course, it seemed to him, was for these brethren to organize as a church upon the basis of their common faith and order, and to be accepted as a new organization by a council which they may call for that purpose in the ordinary manner. That would remove all question in the future. Being thus organized, he did not see that any special stigma would attach to them in consequence of their former connection with the Church of the Puritans. He thought that this Council would prove that there is strength and unity, as well as individual liberty, in Congregationalism.

Rev. C. H. A. Bulkley, of the First Congregational Church, Paterson, N. J., said: "I regret very much, sir, my incompetence to express a positive opinion with regard to this case, from the fact that some peculiarly pressing circumstances prevented me from being here during the whole deliberations of the Council. But I think I have heard enough of the evidence presented, to enable me to approximate toward the right decision. In the first place, I want to make a single remark with regard to the resolution I offered respecting Dr. Cheever's relation to this Church, and the action of this Council toward him. The specific object that I had, was not so much — though that was in part entertained — to express the utmost kindness and do the fullest justice to Dr. Cheever, but to enable ourselves to do justice to the churches which we represent, as well as to our own ministerial relations with him. I remember, in a conversation that I had with him after the other Council, that he, morbidly, as I thought, entertained the idea that there was a certain kind of vindictiveness of feeling toward him on the part of the brethren, which led to the decision, as well as a belief that the decision was on the ground of anti-slavery. I did not believe that to have been so, and I was rejoiced to hear from Dr. Thompson the expression that he had endea-

vored to defend and uphold Dr. Cheever, even to the offending of good friends. I feel, sir, in respect to this, that Dr. Cheever, in his simplicity, and in the confidence of his nature, has given credence to representations made to him which have been false; and, perhaps, in that confidence, has even believed more than was told him; and that there has been a power behind the throne greater than the throne itself, so that Dr. Cheever has been hoodwinked, bamboozled, gulled, and sold.

Now, sir, with regard to this British Mission: in all my conversation with him and with others of the members of his Church, I have not received the very first intimation of the fact that any authority was given to this lady who was sent out, leading me to presume that she went from an official dicta. The idea I entertained was, that the pastor and a few friends of the Church had counseled together and deemed it advisable that funds should be collected. It is a new revelation to me altogether that this evidence gives, that there has been an express authority of the pastor on which she went out to this mission. So far as the collecting for the Church was concerned, I suppose that any member of that church was fully competent to collect this fund any where that he chose, only I think it was an injudicious and impolitic thing to do it without the authority of the Church. The error I conceive to be here, that the Church did not take exception to that mission, and declare it done without any authority on their part. I think they should have summoned at once the pastor and those of the people that were with him, and said that they had done a thing injudicious and impolitic. If they had done this, all this difficulty would have been removed. I am extremely solicitous for Dr. Cheever's sake, for the sake of the Council, for the sake of the Congregational body, that not a peg should be given by which Dr. Cheever should hang a rag of suspicion and accusation, with respect to this question, that it is either personal jealousy and invidiousness toward him, or a question of pro-slavery or anti-slavery that influenced this Council; and I hope that the Council, in its action, will be ready to present this in that light before the public and the churches. I do not think, sir, the statement to be altogether correct, that this evidence presented before us has been one-sided, for, though this has been an *ex-parte* Council, yet the evidence has not been *ex parte*. I hold that the evidence has been fair and equal on both sides. We base our judgment, and solely, upon the documentary evidence which is brought before

us, in the same way as documentary evidence is brought before the Supreme Court. As I understand it, these brethren who have been present and testified, have not testified to any new and additional facts, not contained in these documents, or have only offered a simple explanation of these documents, so that we can understand the whole bearing of the case; and the judgments which we express have been based solely upon the documents which have been brought before us as printed and written, and which are therefore as coming from the other side. I can not conceive how any one can suppose for a single moment that this is one-sided evidence. It is not so; it is fair and equal. We could not form any judgment at all, unless we had had evidence from the other side. Now, sir, I have for a long time sympathized with Dr. Cheever, for many kindnesses done to me, and I have felt that the course of this Church has been unjustifiable, outrageous, abominable, uncongregational, and unconstitutional. I considered it a sort of John Mitchel operation; that John Mitchel who fought and talked for Irish liberty, that he should come to this country, and for gain get a Southern plantation, and should now be a secessionist. The statement which has been mentioned, that this Church is a stench in the nostrils of the churches, I think is not proper. I think that Christ and his disciples were a stench in their time, that Luther and his people were a stench in the nostrils of the English Church, and so are we at the North now a stench in the nostrils of the Southern Church. I think that argument does not apply. Notwithstanding, that there is something that smells bad and that is rotten in Denmark, I will not deny.

I can not go over, nor is it necessary, with the specific complaints that have been made. The principal question now before us, I think, is this: Has the course of this Church been such as to justify us in declaring our opinion, that we, as ministers, and as churches here represented, can not henceforth fellowship with them. Now it is resolved into this simple formula, either they have acted conscientiously and rightfully as a church, or they have not. If they have acted conscientiously and rightfully as a church, then we must recognize them and still fellowship with them; if they have not done so, we can not recognize them, and can not fellowship with them. I think the opinion has been fully and unanimously expressed, that this body has not acted as a church of Christ, and although, according to the conventionalisms of orthodoxy they may have a perfectly pure creed, and their organization may be perfect in its character, though they may, in that sense, be called a church of Christ, yet, I think that, spiritually considered, they have not a shadow of a claim to such a designation. And I would a thousand times rather take into the arms of my fellowship some Unitarian churches and ministers that I know, who are right in heart, but, as we think, wrong in head. I would rather take them a thousand times over, than these men who are right in head and action, so far as orthodoxy is concerned, but wrong in heart; they have the form of orthodoxy without its power and spirit. But yet I have no doubt that there are many members of that Church who are with that majority, who are in the same unhappy predicament with the pastor—that they with him have been hoodwinked, bamboozled, gulled, and sold, thoroughly; and by and by they will come to see—just as Union men in Baltimore and Maryland have come to see—how they have been taken in. I believe we should always strive to exercise the very utmost forbearance toward our Christian brethren. No church and no individual ought to be presumed to be beyond the possibility of repentance and of return. I think that the Council, in their result, should, as briefly and as thoroughly as possible, present this case, lay down the principles of Congregationalism which are clear and succinct, and show to them that they have violated those principles—give them an opportunity to reconsider their action and to reverse it, and allowing them a specific time in which they should do this; then, if they persist in their action, if they will not restore these brethren to their former position and relation to the Church, then the act of this withdrawal of fellowship on our part must go into operation. I think this is the best way. Let them see that we disapprove of their action, give them time to reverse that action; then if, after a fitting time, it is not done, have it understood that these brethren in the minority are set as that church.

In respect to the question, "What is to be done with these brethren?" I should, by all means, if that church shall refuse to reverse their action, advocate the formation of a new church organization, for two reasons. The first is, that nothing should be separated, scattered abroad here and there, for it will be an acknowledgment on their part that they are vanquished, and it will give to the other party the basis on which they may claim that they have gained the victory. I think, while all personal matters should be laid aside, that there are principles involved and consequences to result from the action of this Council, that demand that no such assumption as that should be allowed to them, and no such acknowledgment should be made on the part of this minority; they should be kept together, they should be formed into an organization which shall show that they have life, and strength, and justice on their side; then again, the issue that has been made is, that these brethren are opposed to Dr. Cheever and the Church, on account of their pro-slavery feelings. How can this be refuted in any better way than by constituting these brethren into a new organization, whose expression of opinion, and whose choice, it may be, of a pastor, shall show most distinctly to that church and to the public that they are positively and unequivocally anti-slavery, and that that was not the issue at all which led to this division. I think for these two reasons, sir, that it is very important that this minority should be formed into a new organization, that they should be, after a lapse of time, and after an opportunity given for the reversal of the action of that body, given the privilege of a new organization which shall be the exponent of true anti-slavery principles. I think that this is a process which God has taken, in order to sift and purge the Church of the Puritans, and bring out of it that seed-grain which shall stand on the Congregational mountain-top, which shall be planted and scattered abroad, and the leaves of which shall wave in the breath of liberty, and the seed of which shall be planted every where throughout this city, and nation, and the world.

Rev. W. B. Brown, of the Congregational Church, Newark, N. J., said, the whole of the interest of this matter seems to me to center upon Dr. Cheever and those few who had been associated with him in his earnest and eloquent advocacy of the anti-slavery cause, and it is because of his zeal and sincere interest in that great movement, and because of the deep interest he has felt on that subject, that many of these difficulties have arisen. I have been an interested spectator of what has been transpiring in this church for years. We have all of us been pained and mortified, and all of us in this vicinity have felt that Congregational interests were really imperiled by the difficulties in this church. I have felt the stigma in New-Jersey, standing comparatively alone in the midst of the strongest Presbyterians. Time and again, by pastor and layman, have I been pointed to the transactions of this church as the legitimate fruits of the Congregational and independent policy. And yet I have felt a real sympathy, as I suppose all have felt a real sympathy, with this church in its anti-slavery position. We were in sympathy with the anti-slavery cause, and wished that it might prosper, and so we were ready to bear and forbear; we were ready to make apologies and give extenuations wherever we could, and I have felt inclined, as far as possible, to pass over any imperfections in deportment, for it seemed to me to be right and just to pass them over silently. But yet, I have known for a long time past, things most uncongregational and unchristian in the actions of this church. It has seemed to me that Dr. Cheever and the few who have associated with him have suffered their minds to be completely absorbed in this one idea of anti-slavery interests, and whoever was not in perfect sympathy with them, and whose mind was not heated to the intensity to which theirs had been heated, was not an anti-slavery man, nor was he scarcely a Christian; and all those who stood aloof from them in their one-ideaism were not to be trusted. A few days since I heard a statement to this effect. A gentleman visited one of our insane asylums, and met there a poor one seated on a hobby-horse, rocking himself to and fro, with an earnestness painful to himself and to the beholder. And the gentleman, to raise his spirits, for he seemed sorrowful, said to him:

"Are you fond of horseback riding?"

"No," replied the man, "I never ride horseback, I ride a hobby."

"Well," said the gentleman, "it makes but little difference; it is nearly the same thing."

"No," says the crazy man, "it is not the same thing; for whoever rides on horseback can stop him when he pleases and get off when he pleases; but when one rides a hobby, he can not stop him when he pleases, and he can not get off when he pleases."

The pastor and his associates in this church are on their hobby, and are driven recklessly by the power, and it seems to me that this is the real cause of their extravagances. I have no question but that Dr. Cheever and those associated with him are sincere and earnest, and think themselves to be in the right. I do not believe in the accusations that he is a liar, hypocrite, deceiver — nothing of that — but he is borne away by a kind of influence that he does not distinctly understand, and over which he has no control.

On the evening on which the first great battle of liberty was fought at Fort Sumter, I retired to my bed with deep emotions. I think it was on that same day that I received the communication from this church inviting me and my church to attend this Council; and how it was that in my dreams the two things got mixed up, I am not able to say, but as it seems so expressive of the idea I wish to communicate, I will relate it. In my dream I conceived of myself as being in an immense temple, something like that of St. Peter's in Rome. An immense congregation of tens of thousands were gathered, and far up in the dome on a little platform was Dr. Cheever, standing under the flag of the American republic, and he was haranguing the people on the evil and curse of slavery. He told them they must be ready to make any sacrifice, and die for the cause of liberty. And now, said he, to show my own sincerity, and place before you an example, I will spring from this platform. And so, following the word with the action, he sprang and was dashed upon the pavement. I awoke, saying to myself, He is certainly more patriotic than prudent. And so it has seemed to me in regard to this thing, they are earnest men in what they conceive to be God's work, and they have reached a point where, in regard to this one matter of anti-slavery, I have sometimes questioned as to whether they were quite as responsible as we have been disposed to consider them, and we ought to have charity, for I have met with many a man who seemed to be sharp and keen and clear-headed in every thing but one. I heard of an individual once who was perfectly adequate to transact any kind of business, and on every point but one seemed to be as clear and cool-headed as any one; but he conceived that he had become a miserable tea-pot, and used to stand a-kimbo with this idea, and it was impossible to persuade him to the contrary. Thus much on that point. Now as to the question, What shall these brethren do? On this point I have felt a very deep interest. I remember that within the last few years, since I have been acquainted with New-York and its vicinity, there have been some six or eight Congregational churches—I am not sure as to the number—that have gone on for the time with something like prosperity, and then gone out, so that, with the exception of this Church of the Puritans, we have only one other church in this city standing up prominently, and that is far up town. Now I do not hesitate to say that it has been a great grief to Congregationalists and a great injury to the cause, that these churches have been planted and then extinguished. I chance to live in a region of country where I hear very much concerning these matters, and there is an impression that there is so much looseness, and independence, and want of sympathy among Congregational churches and ministers, that where a church is planted it is left alone to struggle on if it can, and die if it must. I am quite confident that in this city of New-York there ought to be another strong, vigorous Congregational church, and I have not one shadow of doubt, if these brethren shall come together and unite themselves in a Christian Church, that God will bless and prosper them, and another church will be planted here firmly. My wish is, therefore, that another church shall take the place of the Church of the Puritans. As to the question, What shall we do with this Church of the Puritans? I am not prepared to say that if a member of the Church of the Puritans should come to me with a letter of dismission, and I felt that he was a thoroughly sane man on the subject of anti-slavery, and did not come with the purpose of devising things wildly — if he came as an honest Christian man — that I should not accept him; and if any brother in my church should come to me and ask a letter of recommendation to the Church of the Puritans, I should say to him that, with my views of that church, I should advise him not to go there; but if he desired it, I think I should give him the letter of dismission. Wherever you find a real, sincere Christian, you must not debar him from church-membership. I think we are competent to say that the proceedings of this church have been so uncongregational and so unchristian in their character, that we can not any more stand responsible for its acts—that we stand apart and leave it to itself. Thus far I should be glad to go.

Rev. Dr. R. W. Clark, of the South Congregational Church, Brooklyn, N. Y., said: I regard the action of the Church of the Puritans, in suspending six members without any form of charges or complaint being made, or any notice or intimation of trial, as utterly unjustifiable and subversive of all Christian rights. And as there seems to be no hope that these brethren can obtain in the Church of the Puritans any recognition of their just rights, I would vote that they receive, if they desire it, certificates of their good and regular standing in the Church of our Lord Jesus Christ, and be recommended to the fellowship of all true believers. In regard to the Church of the Puritans itself, I would recommend that we withdraw fellowship from it on the ground of its unwillingness to submit any of its difficulties to the decision of an ecclesiastical council, and its disorderly conduct in relation to its members; its course in establishing unscriptural and unreasonable tests of church-membership, and for other reasons that might be specified. Should the aggrieved members desire to be organized into a church, I would vote for such a measure, and cordially extend to them the right hand of fellowship.

Remarks of the Moderator.

The Scribe then took the chair, and Rev. Dr. Sturtevant, the Moderator, said: As to my views in this matter, I do not conceive it to be necessary to review the particular points of this case. It seems to me that, in this respect, the discussion has been thorough and exhaustive. There are, however, a few suggestions that I have to make, bearing on the last two points. I can not entirely concede that the view which has been taken of these two points is, in all respects, as thorough as it should be. At all events, I wish to make a few suggestions. All that I have to say will, as I believe, spring logically from one single position, and that position is, that the party that has assembled this Council is *de jure* and *de facto* the Church of the Puritans, and entitled to all the rights and privileges, even to the name of the Church of the Puritans, although in establishing their claim to that name, should we succeed in doing so, it might possibly prove that they had drawn the elephant in the lottery; nevertheless, I should still claim that the elephant was there; they might dispose of him as they please, but he is there properly. What ground, then, for taking this position? Why, I answer, simply this: I am no lawyer, and make no pretensions to any thing but common-sense in the direction of law, but I take it that law is common-sense, and common-sense, in such a matter as this, is law. Suppose that twelve men are united together in a society holding property subject to certain rights and conditions, and that seven of those twelve vote to dispose of that property, in utter violation of those conditions; and that five adhere to the original conditions of the society. The society now is composed of those five, and the seven are not the society at all. Those five will hold the property in law, and by equity, justice, and common-sense. That Church of the Puritans holds all its rights, privileges, and immunities under certain conditions; those conditions are the constitution of the church, and the constitution of the Church of the Lord Jesus Christ is recognized by that particular church; and that constitution is authority as to terms of membership and rights of membership in the church. Here, now, is a case. In violation of all the forms and of the spirit of law and constitution, six members of this church are, by a majority, declared to be out of the church. That is a violation of those fundamental rights upon which that society holds all it possesses. Now, I say that those six men, and any minority of that church that unite with those six men, are the society. They

are entitled to all the rights of the church and the name of the church; I mean the church considered as a voluntary society. And this matter would apply to the property on Union Square, if the laws of this State were as the laws of some States. I understand that the trustees that hold that property are appointed by the ecclesiastical society, and not by the church; therefore my argument does not go to that extent. But so far as we are concerned merely, it makes no difference. I regard, therefore, the minority, who have called this Council, the Church of the Puritans; and they ought to be so considered and treated in the result of this Council. And had this minority claimed to be the Church of the Puritans, and with such a claim sent forth their call to this Council to recognize them as the Church of the Puritans, I would—as the facts are before me now—I would have voted to sustain them in that claim, and have recognized this Council as a council assembled with the Church of the Puritans. This is true in any case in which the constitution of the society is violated in the dismission of a member, and principles are assumed which are utterly subversive of the constitution, and the minority of the church adheres to the constitution while the majority tramples it under foot. From this point it seems to me that the whole logic of the case is perfectly clear. What shall we do with these brethren from the church? If they do not like the name, Church of the Puritans, let them take another; but I am, after all, averse to admitting that the word Puritan can be so easily and vitally disgraced. It is a word that carries in its very sound noble historic associations that will redeem it from a thousand local disgraces. I did, however, mean to speak on that point; let the brethren use their own discretion. They are the church; if they can stand up and act as the church, let them; if they can not, why, then, let them take letters from the Church of the Puritans to such churches as they please to join. We can recognize these brethren as the church, and they can then dissolve themselves by giving letters. What, then, with the church on Union Square? what has the Council to do? To recognize it as extinct—to recognize it as extinct? There is a great deal said in this Council about withdrawing fellowship. Before I came from home, away on the banks of the Illinois river, I received a warning that we should not lay our hands on the Church of the Puritans, that we should not come together to assume any such dictatorial and legislative powers — the powers that other denominations assume over their particular churches — that we were

to abstain from that. Now I wish to be perfectly understood on that point. I never will vote to withdraw fellowship from any church as long as I believe it to be a church of the Lord Jesus Christ. I never will. I give the right hand of my fellowship to every Presbyterian church in this city, the right hand of my fellowship to every Methodist church in this city, and so on all around the whole evangelical body. I withdraw no fellowship from them; I never will vote to withdraw fellowship from them. And I would not vote to withdraw fellowship from the Church of the Puritans on Union Square, if I believed it to exist, and to be a church of our Lord Jesus Christ.

If I recognized the church on Union Square as still existing, I would never vote to withdraw fellowship. I would vote that the proceedings so and so are not Congregational—that Congregationalism is not responsible for such and such proceedings, and that, as far as churches are related to each other congregationally, this church has, in our judgment, divested itself of its privileges. I would hold myself under solemn obligation to vote so much, because all Congregationalism has suffered wherever the name of Congregationalism is known, by the disorders of the Church of the Puritans, and our enemies all over the land have said: "Aha! aha! so would we have it." They are not to have it so. This Council is not to pronounce, it is not to legislate, is not to adjudicate over that church; but it is to spread these facts before the public, and compare these proceedings with our recognized principles, and to show the public all over the country that the incense of the stench on Union Square is not Congregationalism, but springs from violation of its fundamental principles, and of its constitutional provisions under them. That is what this Council is to do, and just so far as the public will pause, and look, and consider, they will say that it is so. If they will not, but will take things as they merely lie on the surface, they will still continue to lay the disgrace to Congregationalism on Union Square. That we can not help; but we say, so far as men will reason, we will reason with them, and so far as men have got understanding and brains, we will convince them, and we can not furnish arguments and brains both. What is the constitution of the church on Union Square? Is it the constitution of the Lord Jesus Christ? Is it the Gospel — is it Christianity? Oh! no; Dr. Cheever, as the apostle of American anti-slavery on Union Square, supported by the British Aid Mission, is the constitution of the Church of the Puritans. And that is not a Christian church — that is not a

Christian constitution; and, therefore, we should have no hesitation in saying that we do not recognize it. The analogy has been drawn between this defection and defection into Unitarianism, or any form of flagrant error. I do not love, honor, fellowship, defection into flagrant doctrinal error; but if I must make a choice between two bad things, give me apostasy into doctrinal error, rather than apostasy into a violation of practical morality. That last is the apostasy of the church on Union Square, and that I consider the far more serious and terrible of the two.

I wish to say one word also in reference to the philosophy of the whole thing, as it seems to me. How has it been brought about? I am only going to stop for a moment on that point, and then I shall be done. How is it? Are these men rotten at heart —Dr. Cheever and all? No; I am not going to take that position. Here, however, one word a little aside from that. It is all the time assumed, and members of the Council have confessed that they came here with that impression, that there is a pro-slavery faction in the Church of the Puritans, and that the cause of all the difficulty is, that that pro-slavery faction are not willing that Dr. Cheever should preach anti-slavery, and this has gone out all over the country, and it is believed by hundreds that the reason why this trouble exists is, that all Congregational ministers are so pro-slavery, that they are not willing that Dr. Cheever should preach anti-slavery on Union Square. I was in this city at the anniversaries of 1857. I heard Dr. Shepard's address before the Congregational Union, and toward the close of that address I heard Dr. Shepard's address to Dr. Cheever himself, paying him one of the most eloquent compliments I ever listened to, for his bold stand on behalf of the slave, and I heard that thundering burst of applause from all that congregation in hearty sympathy. It expressed the heart of us all — every man of us — it was a compliment to Dr. Cheever for his bold stand in behalf of liberty. At the Congregational collation, when the sainted Dudley A. Tyng paid his compliment to Dr. Cheever, how did that audience break forth into the most tumultuous applause—the enthusiasm surpassed all power of expression. What was it? It was sympathy with Dr. Cheever in the cause of the slave—it was nothing else. I have one more word to add. I knew at that time, and hundreds of Congregationalists in this city knew at that very time, that there were a course of measures being pursued in the Church of the Puritans that seriously threatened the loss of that citadel to the cause of Congregationalism. We then had but a glimpse of it, and said we, one with another: "No man shall strike Dr. Cheever. Dr. Cheever now stands as the representative of anti-slavery, and we will stand around him in one solid phalanx, and no man shall strike him." I appeal to these fathers and brethren if that was not so; I have met it again and again in this city. And now are we to be told that we are all opposed to Dr. Cheever, because he is an anti-slavery man? and are we to be published to the world as miserable pro-slavery men, who dare not speak in the cause? I know that he is absent, but we are present, and these facts are present, and it is fit that they should be spoken.

How has it come about? When Jemima Wilkinson commenced her career, she was perfectly sincere—she really believed that she had a mission from God. She was a pure, simple enthusiast. She thought there was given her a certain mission to accomplish, and it must be accomplished. And she drew around her converts as enthusiastic as herself, and they organized a community; and now the glory of God depended on sustaining that organized community and carrying out her projects, and in order to keep up her credit, she resorted to all the tricks of impostors that can be conceived. That is the way we always do when we assume that we, ourselves, are God's chosen instruments, and that in order to save the world from ruin, our particular system of measures must be kept up. It is saying: "God can not do without us — the Lord can not do without us." American slavery, for instance, can not be abolished unless Dr. Cheever has the citadel on Union Square, to stump from that point. That is the assumption. The end sanctifies the means — that is the philosophy of it. Brethren and fathers, we must not commit this error. We must believe that God's truth, and God's principles, and God's government, are high above all our plans, and submit all to him, and feel that we are lowly and insignificant, and as nothing, and then we may do some little good for God.

The opinions of each member present having been called for and heard, miscellaneous discussion commenced.

Rev. Dr. Bouton, of the Congregational Church, Concord, N. H., said:

With the liberty of the Council, I wish to speak a very few words on what I consider to be the relation of this Council to this particular case, inasmuch as the doctrine just advanced is not as I conceive, with due respect to the Moderator, the Congregational doctrine. A church of Christ is a body of believers in Christ, associated by covenant, for the purpose of maintaining the worship and ordinances of God. It is a fundamental law, that every such Church of Christ shall be governed by a majority of the body, according to the constitution which they have seen fit to adopt — that constitution being, according to their views, in accordance with the New Testament of our Lord and Saviour. Now, it is a sacred and unalterable principle in Congregationalism, that the majority shall govern, and govern according to their own understanding, of the principles of the constitution which they have adopted. Well, suppose that, in the judgment of the minority, that body violate that rule. Then that minority has the right of calling a council to have their difficulties adjusted. First, a mutual council, after which, if it is denied, an *ex-parte* council—and an *ex-parte* council, in Congregationalism, I conceive to be a safety-valve of that body — it is the safety-valve of Congregationalism. That is, if a member, or two or three members are down-trodden and oppressed by the majority, then that minority may appeal for relief to an *ex-parte* council, and get such relief as they are able to give. Now, I find that in all the proceedings of this Church of the Puritans, they have proceeded strictly upon the vote of the majority. The majority rule has never been denied. I highly respect the action of this minority, in that they have never disputed the authority of the majority. Now, the Church of the Puritans, as I understand it, stands on its own firm foundation—it is the Church of the Puritans to-day. It has acted by a majority of its members; they interpreting their own constitution, and act ing according to their own views of right. We say they have acted wrong, but that does not destroy the constitution of the Church of the Puritans — it is still a church. Now, these members, seeking relief from this *ex-parte* council, are just in this position. They are suspended by the action of the majority of a regularly constituted Church of our Lord Jesus Christ. Therefore they are not the Church of the Puritans. They are suspended; they are not finally excommunicated; they may hang on. I take the true Congregational law to be this, that the true position of these members is simply this — it is the right of this *ex-parte* council, as the safety-valve of Congregationalism, to certify to the good character and standing of these members that have been suspended, notwithstanding the action of the majority of the Church of the Puritans. They are still worthy brethren; worthy of recommendation to sister churches, and worthy of the recommendation of this *ex-parte* council to be organized into a new church. That is the true position of the brethren, if I understand Congregationalism. These brethren are in that state of suspension in which they can have no rights of communion and privileges of the Church of the Puritans, to which they have belonged.

Rev. Dr. THOMPSON.—I beg your pardon. This Council is called by a committee, acting as a committee for seventy-six members, among whom are these six who were suspended for asking a council. We are called by seventy persons not suspended, but denied the right of a mutual council, and along with them are six suspended members.

Dr. BOUTON.—Then I hold that the Church of the Puritans had the right, by a majority vote, to refuse a mutual council, and then, that these aggrieved members, cut off or not, have a right to ask the advice of an *ex-parte* council — and this is that council which they have called for their relief. Then I have mentioned the relief that I think we have power to give. I think the church had a right to do what they have done, according to their convictions, the majority vote determining what they consider proper to do.

Dr. BUDINGTON.—Allow me to ask one question. I want to know if Dr. Bouton regards that this church, which denies the followship of the churches, has a right to do that, and leave its Congregationalism intact?

Dr. BOUTON.—I do not understand that they deny the fellowship of the churches by refusing, in a particular case, the call for a mutual council.

Dr. BUDINGTON.—I fully regard the distinct statement of the right of the church to do as it pleases in that sense. But here is church on the platform of Congregational fellowship; it will extend and receive from other evangelical churches that fellowship. I think it is bound to regard the decisions of mutual councils, and to seek the promotion of peace and brotherly love with all the churches of our Lord Jesus Christ. This is the second time that I have been a member of an *ex-parte* council, called to bring peace to that church, and not to that church alone, but to our common Zion. In both instances, these councils, called by name *ex parte*, were, in spirit and in form, as far as the brethren calling them could make them so, mutual councils; and in each instance, the first thing done, by vote of these councils, was to ask the Church to recognize us. They have taken no notice of us whatsoever; they have treated us as if they had no more connection with us, and we no more relation with them, than if we were beasts assembled here. Has the Church of the Puritans a right, as a Congregational church setting down as its standing rule, to deny, with us, the recognition of fellowship?

Dr. Bouton.—I answer, with no hesitation, that they have an entire right to do it, but we have a right to judge of them in regard to that matter. The power of that church lies in the majority of its members, never to be questioned, never to be set aside. By and by the majority abuses the power: it oppresses an individual, or a number of individuals; those oppressed individuals ask for relief, and they seek for it through, first, a mutual council. The Church have a right to say: "We do not need a mutual council — we think still that we do not need a mutual council." They have a right to say this. Then the aggrieved minority ask for an *ex-parte* council. We come, as an *ex-parte* council, to give them relief. We hear their complaint; we say they are aggrieved; we say that the majority have done very wrong; we disapprove of their action; but we have no right to say that that body which has acted wrong, in our judgment, is not a body of our Lord Jesus Christ. They stand there on their own covenant still. By and by we say they have done so wrong that we can not fellowship with them. We give relief to these aggrieved brethren, by certifying to their good standing in the Church of our Lord Jesus Christ.

Dr. Bacon.—I think an appeal was made to me on this point, whether a majority is to govern in a Congregational church. I answer the question, Yes, a majority does govern in all matters, and the minority are bound to submit to the majority in all matters in which the Church acts according to the law of Christ, in all matters that properly come under the jurisdiction of the Church, and in all cases in which the Church proceeds according to the rules of church discipline. It is on that principle, I apprehend, that an *ex-parte* or mutual council revise the proceedings of a church, and say whether the church has violated its authority in those proceedings, and see if it has done what, in the nature of the case, it had no right to do. As I understand the nature of the business which devolves upon the Council, it is this — to see whether the judgment of the Church has any real validity before God; whether the person excommunicated has been really excommunicated by the authority which Christ gave to the Church — if they have excommunicated him for being black, or for any thing which he was not to blame for, then he is not excommunicated; and if they have excommunicated him without taking the first and second private steps, and without admonition, and without trial, then he is not excommunicated; if they have suspended without trial, then he is not suspended.

Dr. Bouton.—One word here. Who is the umpire in this matter, to say whether they have done right or wrong?

Dr. Bacon.—I say Christ is the umpire; I say God is the umpire; I say I am the umpire; every church, every council, is the umpire; it is the independence of one church to do a thing, and the independence of every other church to judge of it. If the Church of the Puritans has a right to judge in this particular case, then the First Church in New-Haven has a right to judge whether the Church of the Puritans judge right or not. That is the principle on which this case rests. That independence is a thing which works all around. Now, it has been assumed in the Church of the Puritans—Dr. Cheever has assumed it—that there was nobody upon earth to be independent but Dr. Cheever; and that has been the principle of proceeding from first to last; whereas, I hold that other folks are independent. I think it is laid down in the books that if a majority does wrong, then the Church does wrong, and the Church is to be censured by the neighboring churches, and ultimately to be cut off from fellowship. If the church violate its covenant, that is, the majority, the act of the majority being the act of the church; if the church violates its covenant with its members, with a minority of seven or five, that it does not destroy the rights of the five; it does not dissolve their covenant with one another, any more than it dissolves their covenant with Christ. Therefore I shall dissent from the view of the venerable father, (Bouton,) as they called him last night, though I remember that I was ahead of him by one class in college. I graduated just one year in advance of him, and I was settled in the ministry just one week before him. He gained on me then, and he has been gaining ever since. I never got venerable yet. (Laughter.) I think that is the key to the whole position here, that the church has no right to do wrong. I think that rule will hold in all cases. No man and no body of men have a right to do wrong.

Dr. Budington.—Is it not wrong to deny a mutual council?

Dr. Bacon.—I think it is most palpably wrong. I think they had not an ecclesiastical right to do it under the circumstances.

Indeed, the rules of that church itself imply that in cases of difficulty, and schism, and separation, there is to be a mutual council. When they institute, as it were, drum-head court-martials, and turn out members neck and crop without opportunity for defense, if ever, under the scope of heaven, there is to be a cause for a mutual council, then is the time. There may be an individual in a church, intractable and quarrelsome, who has fallen into very gross offenses, whom the church excommunicates with a unanimous vote, and the man being factious, contemptuous, and obstinate, demands a mutual council, and the church may rightly say: No, the case is too plain a one; there is no occasion for a mutual council; and if he apply for an *ex-parte* council, he can not get it. Now, here is a case where a church has been rent with divisions and agitations year after year, and the noise of it has gone out into other lands, and here, asking a council, is a half of the church, for the party of the so-called majority have had to send to all parts of the city and neighboring cities, and bring out the infirm and the young to prevent the aggrieved party from carrying their point by vote.

Dr. BUDINGTON.—I will call attention to this fact, that only seventy-one voted against the mutual council, and here are seventy-six asking for it.

Dr. BOUTON repeated, in answer to an inquiry from Rev. Mr. Strieby, his assertion, that it was the right of the Church to assert their right to refuse a mutual council, and it was the right of an *ex-parte* council to judge whether the Church did right in that action.

Dr. BACON called attention to the fact, that in the report presented at the meeting when six members were suspended, of which extracts had been read, the ground was taken that the Church would not have a mutual council in any circumstances, and for the reason alone that the churches did not think as they did — did not believe that Dr. Cheever was the prophet of anti-slavery, as Mohammed is of Mohammedanism. In refusing the council, we think, they did wrong; they think they did right.

Mr. COBB asked who was to decide it.

Dr. BACON said, the universal Church of Christ was to decide it; Christ himself was to decide it, and God was to decide it at the judgment-day.

Dr. BUDINGTON asked, if this Council was unanimous in saying that they did wrong, and seventy-one members of the church said they did right, who, in this country, would have any doubt on the subject?

Dr. Bacon said the church had a right to answer, according to its judgment, whether it would grant a mutual council on the application of the aggrieved party. But the church has no right to judge wrong; no right to overrule, in its judgment, the first principles of Christianity, and of justice, and of common-sense; and all other churches are to judge whether the church, in exercising its right, did wrong. It had no right to do wrong, just as we say that no church has a right to judge that the Lord Jesus Christ is not the Saviour of sinners. So I have a right, he continued, to rule in my own household. I have a right to turn a man out of my house, but I have no right to turn a man out without good reason to do it; and all my neighbors will judge whether I had a good reason or not, and if I had a good reason, they will not admit him to their house. If I turned him out by mere force, without a particle of reason, they will receive him and condemn me. I remember a case in a court once, where a person got very indignant at a colporteur who was obtaining subscribers for books, who had come into his house, and he took him by the ear and led him out with an exercise of force. The court decided that the person used more force than was necessary, and a wrong kind of force, for no human being ought to be pulled by the ear. The church has not a right to do wrong.

Dr. Bouton said the Council had a right to decide whether the church had done right or wrong in the first place, in refusing a mutual council, and in those proceedings which have led to the calling of the Council. We have the same right to give our opinion to these appellants that they have to take the opinion; and that is the same right that Dr. Ball has to write a prescription to a patient who calls on him for advice.

Rev. Dr. Bacon said, if this Council came to a unanimous result in this matter, what church, or intelligent member of a church, from the Atlantic to the Pacific, would doubt as to the justice of that rendering? This Council was to decide the matter, and pronounce its judgment; and from that judgment there lies an appeal to the churches which sent the Council; and from the judgment of the Congregational churches there lies an appeal to the Church catholic of this land, and of all other lands, and to all coming ages; for it is of consequence enough to come up before the tribunal of other ages. That is the theory of ecclesiastical history. The judgment has no right to be any thing else than the expression of the common-sense and Christian conscience of the neighbors about. It is like trial by jury. No man shall be hung unless his neighbors think he ought to be. You must get twelve men from his country to represent, for the time being, public opinion in that box, and if public opinion says the man ought to be hung, it will speak out of that box and say so. If a church has done wrong, and if their neighbors think so, they will say so.

In regard to the withdrawal of fellowship, it was not an act of excommunication; it is not saying that that is not a church of Christ. It is saying that the Church is at present under such errors of faith and practice, that we must keep our communion pure by abstaining from acts of communion with it. Now, there is a First Church in Boston which is out of the communion of the churches. That it is a church, has never been formally denied by any ecclesiastical body. We leave the question whether it is a church to the Master, to whom it belongs. Now, if that church, by and by, comes back to the old foundation, it would be received to the fellowship of the churches with as little difficulty as it went out.

Dr. Thompson said, that if Dr. Bouton, in his remarks concerning the right of the church to do this or that, would substitute the word power, it would probably do away with the confusion. In speaking of the right of the majority to do as they please, he does not wish to carry along with it the idea of moral right.

Dr. Bouton.—I accept that explanation. They have the power of the majority, and we have the power to review their course. There is no question, I suppose, as to the wickedness of the course of the Church of the Puritans, and the moral judgment with reference to these things.

A committee, consisting of Rev. E. P. Gulliver, Judge H. W. Taylor, Rev. Dr. W. J. Budington, Rev. Samuel Walcott, and to which the Moderator was added, was appointed to draft a paper, to be presented to the Council, embodying the result of the Council.

After considerable more casual discussion and comparing of views, the Council adjourned until Monday afternoon, then to hear the report of the committee appointed to draft the result of the Council.

MONDAY AFTERNOON SESSION.

After the usual prayer at the commencement of each day's session, the draft of a result of the Council, by the committee appointed to this office, was presented by Rev. Mr. Gulliver.

Persons not members of the Council were requested to leave the room.

The Report was then read by Mr. Gulliver.

Lengthy remarks were made by many members of the council, in regard to the ecclesiastical principles involved in the document, and suggesting minor changes and amendments. Dr. Bouton was added to the committee on the result of the Council.

EVENING SESSION.

The report of the Committee was read, section by section, and verbal corrections and improvements suggested and made.

Various substitutes and amendments to the report were adopted, making the statement of facts and of the judgment of the Council, in view of the facts, more explicit, and in accordance with the views of members.

TUESDAY MORNING SESSION.

After prayer the result of the Council was finally read, as corrected, and fully approved by every member of the Council present, as follows:

RESULT OF COUNCIL.

The Ecclesiastical Council, called by seventy-six members of the Church of the Puritans, in the city of New-York,* to consider certain alleged grievances suffered by them at the hands of the majority of that Church; also to determine whether that Church has not, by its general policy, so completely and persistently violated the fundamental principles of Congregational order as to have forfeited its claim to the fellowship of our churches; and also to advise the aggrieved members concerning the expediency of their being constituted and recognized as a Church of Christ, after a full, deliberate, and prayerful examination of the subject-matter submitted to them, *unanimously* came to the following

RESULT:

The Council, upon assembling, found evidence that the aggrieved members had not resorted to an *ex-parte* council until, according to Congregational usage, they

* Six of the number who united in the letter missive, having received letters of dismission from the Church of the Puritans, have united with the church to which they were recommended, leaving but seventy who await the action of this Council; and, in speaking of the complainants in the case, we refer exclusively to these seventy.

had sought the assent of the Church to the calling of a mutual council—which request had been denied. Thereupon the Council appointed a committee to communicate with the Church of the Puritans, through its officers, and advised it to accept the Council as a mutual council, and if this invitation should be declined, to meet the Council through a committee, and furnish such information as might be wanted. They were also requested to allow us the use of the church records. The officers of the Church, after consultation, notified us that they had no authority to act in the premises, and neither appeared nor furnished the records.

The question of the expediency of dissolving the postoral relation subsisting between the Rev. George B. Cheever, D.D., and the Church of the Puritans, was intended to be submitted to a mutual council, as proposed to the church by the complainants, and therefore that question was stated in the specifications laid before the Council; that the Council declined to entertain that question at all, and also requested the complainants to confine their statements to the character and doings of the church, and to avoid, as far as possible, all reference to the character and doings of the Pastor, now absent and unable to answer for himself.

It appeared, from the investigations which followed, that the most important points in the case rest upon documentary evidence, and upon public and undisputed acts of the church and its officers. The Council, therefore, find themselves relieved in a great degree from the embarrassment which would have been caused by a strictly *ex-parte* examination, and are able to base their result, in great part, upon the evidence of documents proceeding from the party which declines to appear in the case.

We find the following facts fully proved:

1. That an attempt was commenced in February, 1859, by a few members of the church, to obtain a large fund in Great Britain to meet the current expenses of the church, or, as an alternative, to establish another church.

2. That this movement was unauthorized by the Church or Society, and unknown to them until the November following.

3. That the pecuniary ability of the Society at that period was fully adequate to meet its own expenses, as appears from the fact that, although the annual expenses are less than seven thousand dollars, during the first four months of the year 1859 between seven and eight thousand dollars were raised by the congregation for the removal of the floating debt, and for various other purposes, in addition to the ordinary expenses.

4. That in May, 1859, at the very time that the appeal for aid in Great Britain was in progress, the Society, by the above special subscription, was freed from debt.

5. That the funds obtained were to be placed in the hands of the Pastor of the Church, and of a committee to be selected by him—their successors to be chosen by themselves, without any responsibility to the Church or Society.

6. That the object of this arrangement, in the words of its authors, was "to sustain the ministry of Dr. Cheever in this edifice, if possible; if not, in some other," and that they declined to place the funds under the control of the Church, in consequence of "some doubts as to the permanence of our majority," and also because they were aware that "a large and influential minority, from the nature of the case, would bitterly oppose the measure."

7. That notwithstanding this avowed design to create a money power independent of the Church, and possibly hostile to it, the British Aid Mission was planned

and prosecuted in the name and behalf of the Church, the credentials of Miss Johnstone containing the following language:

"Miss J. visits Great Britain on a mission connected with the interests *of this Church.*" "Miss J. has undertaken to visit Great Britain for the purpose of procuring funds *for the benefit of the Church of the Puritans in this city.*"

8. That Miss Elizabeth Johnstone, who was employed to prosecute the British Aid Mission, was suffered to enter upon it with but a partial knowledge of its plan and objects, and with wrong impressions concerning the pecuniary ability of the Church, and thus was allowed unwittingly to make representations concerning it not in accordance with truth, and to place herself in a false position both at home and abroad.

9. That while this concealment was practiced toward the British public, a similar concealment was practiced toward the parties in interest at home, Miss Johnstone being instructed to keep her proceedings as private as possible, "on account of the clamor which would be raised by our enemies," both donors and ostensible beneficiaries being thus blinded as to these important proceedings, the facts becoming known at last only through the publication of a private letter in a daily newspaper.

10. That all these proceedings concerning the British Mission were fully indorsed and justified by the Church, by formal vote in November, 1859; though by a very small majority.

11. That the Church have allowed tests to be used in admitting members other than those affecting the Christian character of the applicants, with the avowed purpose of constituting not a simple church of Christ, but an organization which should sustain certain men and measures.

12. That the Church has allowed its officers, members, and committees, to represent that all who, for any cause, objected to the course of the majority, were prompted by pro-slavery sentiments, though this was repeatedly and constantly denied by them, and contradicted by their antecedents and present position on that subject.

13. That the Church, in its public meetings and in the reports of its committees, allowed the minority to be stigmatized as "schismatics," "covenant-breakers," and "conspirators," simply because they opposed the course of the majority, although they had never proposed to disregard its decision in any manner which can properly be characterized as schismatic.

14. That the Church regarded and treated an expression of dissent from the policy of the Pastor as only a factious, selfish, and unscrupulous opposition should be regarded and treated.

15. That the Church have repeatedly disregarded their own standing rules in their treatment of the aggrieved parties, and openly justified this course upon the plea that it was necessary in self-defense.

16. That the Church received Mr. T. J. Hall in an irregular manner, without allowing a presentation of objections to his admission, and while a serious difficulty remained unsettled between himself and members of the Church.

17. That charges having been presented to the Church against Mr. Charles Abernethy, in their superficial aspect seriously affecting his Christian character and standing, but in their substance groundless, and evidently so deemed by the Prudential Committee, and the truth of which he immediately and peremptorily denied, repeatedly demanding a speedy trial thereupon, the Church postponed the trial for nearly six months, leaving him under the public reproach of the accusation without

opportunity of defense, and have to this day neither granted him the trial nor withdrawn the charges.

18. That the request made for a mutual council by seventy-six members of the Church, was refused by the Church in circumstances peculiarly demanding, according to the usages of our churches, the calling of such a council.

19. That immediately upon the refusal of the application for a mutual council, six of the applicants—namely: E. W. Chester, Charles Abernethy, C. R. Harvey, George H. White, Thomas Rigney, and Joel Blackmer—were "suspended from all the rights and privileges of membership in the Church, until the Church take other action in the premises," without the offering of any charges or complaint, without any notice of trial, and without any fair opportunity for defense or protest.

20. That the Church, in its public documents and in the general style of remarks in its meetings, has characterized its sister churches and their pastors who did not approve the special measures and peculiar speech of its pastor, as friendly to slavery, or unfaithful in bearing testimony against it.

In this statement the Council have aimed to give the prominent facts in the case in their simplest form. The testimony concerning the circumstances accompanying these transactions, and the spirit and measures of the dominant party in the Church, unfolded to the Council a history, the parallel of which can scarcely be found in all the annals of our churches. Words can not adequately express the shame we have felt that a church, calling itself by the name of the revered Puritans, and identified in the eyes of the public with the Congregational faith and order, and claiming to be the especial champion of human rights, should have exhibited, in this high place of the national metropolis, such scenes of disorder, such disregard of the sacred rights of the household of faith, and such wanton violation of the laws which Christ has laid down for the government of his churches. We find consolation only in the assurance that He who maketh the wrath of man to praise him, will make this sad example the means of strengthening the conviction throughout our churches, already so deeply rooted in the minds of the true sons of the Pilgrims, that the order of Christ's house can only be enjoyed by a strict and conscientious observance of all the laws for the intercourse of the Christian brotherhood, which Christ has ordained.

Having now ascertained the facts in the case, as presented in the testimony and documents, with the exception of those relating personally to the Pastor, the Council proceeds to consider the questions propounded to them by the complainants.

These are mainly two. The first has reference to the course which should be adopted by the churches of the Congregational order toward the Church of the Puritans. The second, to the course which should be taken by the aggrieved brethren concerning their future church relations.

The first of these questions is propounded to the Council in the following words:

"Whether, in view of all the facts and considerations to be brought to their notice, in the examination of these complaints, the interests of the Christian Church do not require that the fellowship of the churches be withdrawn from the Church of the Puritans, and it be declared no longer in connection with the Congregational body."

It will be well understood by all Congregationalists, that the only action which the Council can take concerning the withdrawal of fellowship here mentioned, is of an advisory character. We can give our opinions and the reasons for them. But it will remain for each church to determine for itself, in view of all the facts, whether or not it will adopt our opinions and follow our advice.

The Council, of course, does not assume to act for "the Congregational body."

We see but one course left for our churches. We must withdraw from this church which has virtually withdrawn from us. We must not allow ourselves to be held responsible any longer for the conduct of a church which rejects our principles, spurns our advice, and refuses to redress the grievances of brethren whom we honor and love.

We, therefore, recommend to the churches of the Congregational order that, in such way as shall be accordant with the principles of our platforms and usages, they withdraw from the Church of the Puritains the fellowship of the churches, until it shall recede from its present position, and give evidence of a return to the spirit of Christ and to the order of the Congregational churches.

In respect to the aggrieved members, the Council do, notwithstanding the action of the Church of the Puritans, recognize them as worthy members of the body of Christ; and recommend that, with others who may associate with them, they either be constituted in due form a distinct church, or received into sister churches as they shall prefer. And the scribe of this Council is hereby authorized to give certificates of good standing to such of them as shall apply to him for the same previous to December 1, 1861.

In conclusion, the Council would distinctly and emphatically state that the difficulties and grievances which have passed under their review, have involved no issue between slavery and anti-slavery, but have arisen wholly from the violation by the majority of the Church, of the fundamental principles of church order, and of the most sacred rights of individual members. The Council feel, therefore, that in this result they are vindicating not only Congregationalism, but the cause of anti-slavery, from the reproach brought upon it by the proceedings of the Church of the Puritans. They also express their approbation of the Christian patience and forbearance with which the aggrieved brethren have endured manifold wrongs, and the fidelity with which they have maintained the principles of church order and of Christian duty committed to their trust; and affectionately and earnestly exhort them to continue in the future as they have been in the past, faithful to the kingdom of Christ, to the interests of Congregationalism, and to the cause of anti-slavery, notwithstanding the grievances to which they have been subjected in the name of both. Should they decide to organize themselves into a distinct church, we counsel them to profit by this experience, and to make it a church which shall not only defend the rights of the enslaved, but also the rights of its own members; which shall not only vindicate the principle of the essential independency of every individual church, but shall also recognize the other great principle of Congregationalism—the duty of every church to advise with its sister churches in all matters of common interest, and to give a due respect to their counsels and opinions.

With this exposition of the conclusions to which we have been brought, we leave this painful matter to the revisal of our Christian brethren, and to the disposal of the great Head of the Church.

At the request of the Scribe, a committee was appointed to prepare a form of the letter of recommendation indicated in the Result. Dr. Bouton and the Scribe were appointed for this purpose, who prepared a form, which was submitted and adopted.

The doors were then thrown open, and the complainants called in to hear the result of the Council.

Mr. CHESTER, on behalf of the Committee of the complainants, expressed their thanks for the kindness and patience of the Council, and the interest they had manifested in the affairs which had so deeply interested the complainants.

In answer to inquiries, an expression of their views was heard from a number of the complainants as to their future action.

A resolution was adopted that a committee of five be appointed to recognize the brethren calling this Council, and such as may unite with them, as a church of the Lord Jesus Christ, in communion with Congregational churches, if the brethren should desire it.

The following persons were appointed on that committee by nomination: Rev. Drs. Thompson, Dutton, and Budington, and Rev. Messrs. Stone and Elliott, and their delegates.

Prayer was then offered by the Moderator, after which the Council adjourned *sine die.*

The Committee superintending the publication of these proceedings, have recently had their attention directed to the two letters which follow, which have appeared in a London journal of respectability and influence. These letters present so concisely the opposite views entertained on this subject, and come with so much authority, the one from the Pastor of the Church of the Puritans, and the other from the distinguished Moderator of the Council, that neither excuse for their insertion, nor comment upon their statements and temper, seem to be needed.

The first is from *The Patriot* of August 1st, 1861; the second from the same paper of September 26th, 1861.

THE REV. DR. CHEEVER AND THE CHURCH OF THE PURITANS.

TO THE EDITOR OF THE PATRIOT:

SIR: An article in regard to the Church of the Puritans, of which I am the pastor, having been inserted from an American newspaper in your journal, adapted to produce a false and injurious impression, it is, perhaps, but justice to the friends of the church in this country, and of the cause of emancipation, in behalf of which it has been called to suffer, that some explanation of its position be presented in your columns. I shall be greatly obliged if you will have the kindness to give place to the following remarks, along with the letter from President Blanchard of America.

I am, Sir, yours truly,

GEORGE B. CHEEVER.

LONDON, July 26th.

The Church of the Puritans has for a number of years been distinguished for the earnestness and faithfulness of its struggle against Slavery, at the cost of an incessant conflict with a hostile minority. That church established a monthly concert of prayer for the enslaved, at a time when to adopt such a measure was to render itself a byword and a scorn in the community. That church proclaimed itself an Abolition church at the cost of a conflict within, and almost universal hatred and opposition from without, such as few churches have ever survived. The character of the preaching on the subject of Slavery, which they sustained against such fierce hostility, may be learned from the work of their pastor, entitled *God against Slavery*, and from his last work on the *Guilt of Slavery and Crime of Slaveholding*. Such faithfulness on the part of the church was of itself a rebuke of the silence or complicity and time-serving of other churches not willing to take any active measures against Slavery, nor to be regarded as Abolitionists, yet professing to be Anti-slavery, and enraged that they should be accused of being Pro-slavery. Now that the war has been inaugurated for the Union, and Abolitionism has become almost popular, the hatred and hostility are still continued by the leaders of the *ex parte* Council against the Church of the Puritans. While the church were engaged in the thickest of the fight against Slavery, their enemies have stabbed us from behind; but now that the conflict is popular, they take the very standard which we had unfurled and defended, and themselves occupy the position, over our dead bodies, which we had conquered. Not a few ministers are now busy in preaching sermons in behalf of the Union and of the war to put down this rebellion against the Government, who never opened their lips to denounce Slavery as a sin against God, or to demand freedom for the enslaved in God's name. Those who have heretofore opposed Abolitionism, and forbidden the agitation of the subject of Slavery in the pulpits and churches, are now preaching war against the South as rebels. And it is a most wonderful and wanton cruelty, for a church that confessedly for years has been foremost among the most faithful churches of the land in the moral battle against Slavery, now to be insulted and trampled down by ministers and churches that, withholding themselves from that battle while it was unpopular, throw themselves into the support of the popular war, and now for the first time speak out.

It is impossible to understand this conflict without knowing the difference between mere Anti-slavery and Abolitionism, the profession of the former being universally popular, but of the latter almost universally abhorred and persecuted. Men profess to be Anti-slavery who have no idea of interfering with Slavery at the South in the slaveholding States, and who dread and abhor Abolitionism, and will not suffer the sin of Slavery to be preached against, or the question of its abolition agitated in the churches. Consequently the very men that hate Abolitionism, and would rend any church asunder rather than permit it to be an Abolition church, can at the very same time declare themselves good Anti-slavery men, and affirm that no Anti-slavery issue is involved in their opposition against the church. There is a most bitter opposition against the Church Anti-Slavery Society in America, simply because it has thrown itself on the fundamental truth, by God's word, that slaveholding is in itself sinful. There is the same opposition against the Church of the Puritans, because it carries out and applies that doctrine, and has sought support from British churches in maintaining it; and therefore the pastor of the church has been pursued with relentless hostility, and the effort is still continued to drive him from his post of power in the heart of the city of New-York.

And since the pastor's absence from the country, the trustees of his own church, in answer to the protest against their appeal to Great Britain, did resolve, among other particulars, "That we find the reason why such an appeal abroad is necessary in the fact that our churches, as a body, will not countenance or support a Gospel which proclaims slaveholding a crime and sin to be abolished and exterminated, and that we believe that any church in the Republic, which earnestly and persistently takes sides with the oppressed against the oppressor, will be denounced by its fellow-churches, as having departed from the Gospel of peace and love, and as being given over to fanaticism, and that the inevitable fate of such a church is to be shorn of its wealthy members, robbed of its support, persecuted and defamed." All this, while the profession of Anti-slavery principle, according to its ordinary character, (the mere opposition against the extension of Slavery,) was extremely popular. Almost every church professed to be Anti-slavery, and no such church or minister was ever opposed for such Anti-slavery profession, provided they denounced Abolitionists and Abolition. Now, since the war against the South, and the union of the North in that war, all is changed, and the churches and the ministers who, one year ago were opposed to Abolitionism, and to the preaching of its doctrines, are now anxious to clear themselves of the reproach of such opposition. Yet multitudes of ministers have been driven from their churches for no other cause or crime than that of having preached against slaveholding as sinful, and demanded immediate abolition. The case of the Rev. Dudley Tyng, of Philadelphia, is an instance in point, but a hundred others might be given in the Northern States. The Pro-slavery character of many of the churches and ministers, until within a year, and their opposition against all agitation of the subject, even while stoutly defending themselves as being Anti-slavery, has been notorious. The *Congregationalist* itself, is the very paper that, more than a year ago, published a defense of the Congregational churches, against the charge of being extreme and fanatical, against any suspicion of Abolitionism, and entered into a computation for the purpose of showing how groundless was this charge, declaring that of all the sermons preached by the thirteen hundred Congregationalist ministers during the last ten years, not more than one tenth of one per cent had any allusion whatever to the subject of Slavery.

The *Congregationalist* is the paper that has uttered the calumny against the church and its pastor, of there being other reasons than Slavery for the opposition of the minority against the pastor, and other reasons, consequently, for the division and conflict within the church. This calumny, it is true, is put in the form of an innuendo, plainly because there was no reason ever given, or pretended, for such opposition and conflict, except only the Abolitionism of the church and pastor, and the measures adopted by them, necessarily, in defense of their rights and of the cause of freedom and truth in this great struggle. Had there existed any other reasons, it is plain that the enemies of the church and pastor, in the *ex-parte* Council, as well as out of it, would have brought them forward. But none have even been insinuated, and it is well known that the abolition efforts of the church and pastor, and their persistent earnestness in them, are the whole and sole cause of the conflict. When, therefore, the *ex-parte* Council declare that no Anti-slavery issue is involved, they are careful not to intimate that no Abolition issue is involved, for that is the hinge of the whole matter, and the Abolitionism and Abolition measures of the church and pastor were the ground of the opposition of the Council.

In the whole progress of the recent effort against the church and pastor in New-York, the minority acting against the church, and the leaders of that minority, whose cause the *ex parte* Council espoused, have disclaimed any opposition against the pastor, except on the ground of what is called the British Mission, and the efforts of church and pastor in support of that, especially the suspension from church membership of six leaders of the disorderly faction in the church. The authors of the protest against that mission, signed by some forty persons, and published widely by them in this country, for the avowed purpose of preventing its success here, do not mention any other reasons for their opposition, and were always careful to affirm that they were not opposed to the pastor, and have not desired his removal, but, on the contrary, were able and willing to sustain both him and the church if they would abandon that British Mission, and permit those who opposed it to bear rule. The *Independent* itself, at the very time of the pastor's departure for Europe, and while denouncing his church for its appeal to Great Britain, commended him to the admiration of the churches of Great Britain, as being a worthy representative of the best Anti-slavery principles of the churches of New-England! The conflict against his church on account of its Abolitionism, had been going on for years, and the progress of it is recorded in the annals of the *Independent* itself, in which newspaper he has for years defended the cause of Abolitionism, and proclaimed its doctrines, and called upon the churches and the ministry to espouse and apply them with the word of God.

The following letter addressed to Dr. Cheever, from President Blanchard of Illinois, written after attending the *ex-parte* Council in New-York, will go far toward the removal of the wrong impression produced by that Council — a Council representing and espousing only the opposing minority in the church, and called together for the purpose of shielding the suspended members from the effect of church discipline—a Council having not the slightest authority over the church, nor the least right to interfere in its affairs, but yet attempting to usurp such authority, and presuming upon such interference:

"DEAR BROTHER: I am here from the West to attend the anniversaries, and find in session here, a Council called *ex parte*, by certain suspended members of the Church of the Puritans, of which you are pastor. Living so far west, I have heretofore given the slightest possible attention to the circumstances growing out of the intensity of your testimony against the slave-power, and particularly against its influence over the churches of this country.

"I have attended one session of this Council, and have conversed with your friends here, and as I was in 1843 the American Vice-President of the World's Anti-Slavery Convention, and preached for a few Sabbaths in some of the churches of London, where some ministering brethren may still recollect me, it has occurred to me that my testimony and judgment, from this place, and at this time, may be of some use, by assuring you that multitudes in our country sympathize with you, and, perhaps, may strengthen your hands, and encourage your friends in Europe to aid you in your mission to relieve the Church of the Puritans from pecuniary embarrassment, to which it is subjected through no fault of yours.

"Dr. Leonard Bacon, of New-Haven, was counsel for the appellants in this Council; and in order that our English brethren may know precisely how he differs from us, I send the following plain and pointed quotation from a speech of his at a meeting of the American Board, in Brooklyn, near this city, a few years since, which, so far as I know, expresses his sentiments to-day. Dr. Bacon said:

"'He would like the report better, if it contained a distinct avowal that slaveholding is not a sin in itself, in such a sense as to disqualify a man for church-membership.'

"Condemning 'Slavery' as a 'system,' with great force of language, he yet holds that slaveholding is no disqualification for church-membership, and, of course, as systems of wrong can not repent, his doctrine is either practically nugatory, or it operates to divert condemnation from slaveholding and slaveholders, and thus practically shelters the system which he condemns.

"The influence of Dr. Bacon is, on other accounts, deservedly extensive in this country, and his post as Editor of the *Independent*, makes it extensive also in Europe. I believe him to be in error on the subject of slaveholding, and that his erroneous position, and your testimony against that position, have ranged his influence, and that of a large number of ministers whom he influences, against your position and course. But, while very many ministers are with him, and influence their people more or less, it is my opinion that if the members of the Congregational churches throughout the country were empaneled, at least forty-nine in every fifty of them would approve of your position, and condemn his; and I have a somewhat extensive acquaintance with the sentiment of Congregationalists in this country, East and West.

"There are divers small matters, as will always be the case, thrown into this contention. It is not difficult, in the absence of a pastor, to find or make discontented members in his church; and I condemn the calling of this *ex-parte* Council, at the instance of suspended members, in your absence. And I strongly condemn the sentiments which I have heard freely uttered by the Chairman and other members of the Council, condemning you, (in your absence from the country, and your church, which was not represented there,) for alleged irregularities of church action, as though such things were new or unusual, with an absent pastor, in an agitated church.

"But I rejoice that in these unhappy difficulties, not the slightest imputation has ventured to appear upon the purity of your character as a minister or as a man.

"In the great commercial headquarters of Slavery, I can understand how Pro-slavery wealth and influence may infect some of your own members. But I rejoice that the great majority of them appreciate your labors, and love your person with a devotion only intensified by the terrible ordeal through which you are called to pass, in the opposition of ministers, whose position you have condemned, and also of those sincere but lesser minds, more or less of whom are always drawn into such sinister movements by superior intellectual power.

"I pray that Christ will be with you, and incline brethren in that country which has, by God's help, delivered itself from the darkening and corrupting influence of the slave system, to grant you pecuniary aid to place the Church of the Puritans, so central in this great metropolis, beyond embarrassment. Wishing you grace and peace in Christ, Your friend and brother,

"J. Blanchard,

"President of Wheaton College,

"New-York, May 6th, 1861. Illinois, U. S. America."

To the Editor of the Patriot:

Sir: It seems due to the cause of truth, and to a just understanding of the present great American crisis, that some reply should be made to an article which appears in your issue of August 1st, from the Rev. Dr. Cheever and President Blanchard.

Dr. Cheever's article is certainly fitted, I do not say it was intended, to make the impression that the late *ex-parte* Council was called by a pro-slavery minority in the Church of the Puritans, disaffected toward the Pastor on account of his exemplary fidelity to the cause of the enslaved. President Blanchard's letter seems to have been introduced as the testimony of an eye-witness confirming the same impression. It is painful to deny representations of matters of fact, coming from two well-known ministers of the Gospel. But necessity compels it. President Blanchard's testimony is not that of an eye-witness of the proceedings of the

Council. The sessions of that body opened on the 2d of May, and terminated on the 7th. Mr. Blanchard was only present a few moments at the close of the session on the 7th, and heard none of the proper deliberations of the body. He is no more qualified to testify on the subject than he would have been if he had remained at Wheaton College.

The impression which the two reverend gentlemen have made is certainly most erroneous and cruelly unjust. If Dr. Cheever will interrogate his own memory, he will find indelibly recorded there a grateful sense of the strong and enduring moral support in his efforts in the cause of the oppressed which he has received from these men whom he now stigmatizes as a "hostile minority." It is unjust, because it is untrue, to represent these men as hostile to Dr. Cheever as an "Abolitionist." They have made no attack upon Dr. Cheever at all. The Council has made none. The minority complain of the action of the Church of the Puritans. The grounds of their complaint are all set forth in the "Result of the Council." This Result was published in the *Independent* of May 16th, and the substance of it has, I believe, been laid before your readers. The Council founded its disapprobation of the doings of the Church of the Puritans, on twenty distinct allegations of matters of fact, not one of which sustained any relation whatever either to "Anti-slavery" or "Abolitionism." To this "Result" the majority now dominant in the Church of the Puritans has officially replied. But in their reply they have not denied one important statement of fact put forth by the Council. They meet the complaints of the aggrieved minority, not by denying the facts which they allege, but by the claim that in a Congregational church the majority governs, and may do what it pleases. We appeal to the Christian brotherhood in this and other lands, whether this reply is satisfactory. We of the Council should be among the last men in the world to set any ecclesiastical authority on earth above the decisions of a majority of the brotherhood in a Christian church. But has such a majority, therefore, a right to do whatever it pleases? Is it not amenable to the laws of Christ? Has not the feeblest member rights, which it is bound to respect? May the majority of a church, if it pleases, suspend from the privileges of the church six of its leading members, without any charges, without citation, and without any trial? And when fully one third of the entire living membership of the church protests against such a proceeding, and asks for a friendly arbitration, to aid in adjusting the difficulty, have their views no claim to consideration and a hearing? Is it a sufficient answer to such a minority to tell them to be silent, the majority governs? If such are the principles of Congregational polity, who will hereafter join a Congregational church?

Or again, has the majority of a church a right to entertain charges against a brother, deeply affecting his moral and religious character, and yet for months refuse him any hearing, though he wholly and earnestly denies the truth of the charges, and finally, after many months of delay, to suspend him from the privileges of the church, without any trial at all? The Christian public will never admit that such proceedings can find any justification in the independence of a church of Christ, or of any other ecclesiastical authority. We of the Council admit that we have, and desire to have, no authority over a church which does such things. To the Master that church must answer it. But we are shocked by such acts, done by a body claiming to be a church of Christ. We believe they admit of no justification, and that the Christian public ought to say to a minority thus aggrieved: "You have our sympathy and our fellowship: we regard you as greatly injured and the church by which you have been thus arbitrarily treated, as having sinned grievously against the law of Christ and the household of faith."

As, therefore, the majority in their reply to the "Result of the Council," have not denied the facts alleged by the minority and the Council, the public is henceforth to regard these facts as admitted by the special friends of Dr. Cheever in the Church of the Puritans, and to judge for themselves, whether these admitted facts justify the unfavorable opinions expressed by the Council, not respecting the character of Dr. Cheever, but the acts of the Church of the Puritans. That church did suspend from its privileges six leading members, without citation or trial. They did refuse to grant these brethren any redress or relief by friendly arbitration, when requested to do so by one third of the living membership of the Church. They did entertain charges seriously affecting the moral and Christian character of Mr. Charles Abernethy, which he asserted to be utterly false, and yet for many months refused him any hearing; and, finally, suspended him from the privileges of the church, without any trial on these or any other charges.

The Council did express its strong disapprobation of these and of many other disorderly, arbitrary, and unrighteous acts of the Church of the Puritans, and advised all sister churches to treat such acts as of no force or validity against the injured minority, and not to hold fellowship with that church, till it shall give evidence of repentance. The Council did not try, much less did it condemn, Dr. Cheever. It did not assume to exercise any ecclesiastical power whatever over the Church or its Pastor. It simply examined the matters submitted to it by certain aggrieved members, and expressed its judgment of the same to the Christian public.

The true position of the minority which called the *ex-parte* Council is, therefore, obvious enough. They are not, as Dr. Cheever seems to charge, "hostile" to the "Abolitionism" of the Church of the Puritans, or of its Pastor. They are not "hostile" to any thing, except to the arbitrary acts of the Church, which are set forth in the "Result of Council," not one of which has any relation to "Anti-slavery" or "Abolitionism." Of these acts they complain, and through the Council appeal to the Christian public for sympathy and recognition, when unjustly cast off by the Church.

Again, Messrs. Cheever and Blanchard make the impression that the Council was composed of Pro-slavery men — men who "never opened their lips to denounce slavery as a sin against God" — and that the whole proceeding was instigated by hatred of Dr. Cheever and his Church, for their fidelity in the cause of freedom. It is my solemn conviction, that such an impression is utterly untrue in respect to every member of the Council. Such a statement respecting any member of that Council who has a public reputation, (and most of its members have a public reputation,) would strike all right-minded Christian people in this country as false and slanderous, and would injure the Christian reputation of no one, except of the man who should deliberately make it. I am acquainted with no member of that Council, who has not, in the struggles of the last ten years, done his utmost to uphold and countenance Dr. Cheever in his boldest attacks upon the domineering slave power, and to protect him from his enemies.

If Dr. Cheever and President Blanchard do not know this, it is because they have been too much engrossed with the thought of their own bravery and prowess in this moral war, to do justice to their companions and fellow-soldiers in the fight.

Complaints are made because the Council was held in Dr. Cheever's absence

But what has this to do with the question? The Council was not called to sit in judgment on Dr. Cheever, or any of his acts, but only on the known, and now admitted, acts of the Church of the Puritans. If a church arbitrarily suspends six of its members from the privileges of the church, must those six members seek no vindication of their rights, and no redress of their wrongs, because the pastor is sojourning for an indefinite period on the other side of the Atlantic? Especially when the arbitrary act of excision was done in the Pastor's absence, and may be presumed to have been countenanced by his approbation and advice.

President Blanchard says: "I strongly condemn the sentiments which I have heard freely uttered by the Chairman and other members of the Council, condemning you, (in your absence from the country and your church, which was not represented there,) for alleged irregularities of church action," etc. Does the President of Wheaton mean that he condemns the Chairman and other members of the Council, for condemning such "irregularities of church action" as those specified in the "Result of Council," and admitted as matters of fact by Dr. Cheever's special friends? Does he mean that it is wrong to condemn such "church action," whether it be that of the Church of the Puritans or of any other church, whether its pastor be at the time absent or present, in Europe or in America? Does he mean that to condemn such church action is to speak evil of Dr. Cheever? If this is what he means, it will be very hard for many of us on this side of the Atlantic to agree with him. It will seem to us that such church action is to be condemned without much respect to the presence or the absence of the pastor.

The language employed by Dr. Cheever and President Blanchard, is peculiarly fitted to make an erroneous and mischievous impression on the English mind, in relation to the great American crisis. If that had been true of the American churches and ministers which they seemed to represent, the present crisis of our national history would not have existed. The slave-power would still have been holding the nation in its grasp. The Union would have still existed unbroken and unassailed, but utterly perverted from the original designs for which it was created, into an iniquitous league for treading down a continent under the iron heel of slavery. It has long been the settled purpose of the Southern slave-power to govern the nation in the interest of Slavery; to silence by the terrors of the Lynch-court and the bowie-knife, every utterance against that iniquitous system, and in favor of the universal rights of man, from the St. Lawrence to the Rio Grande. In that monstrous scheme of iniquity they have been foiled and defeated by the solemn protest of the churches, the ministers, the friends of freedom and the rights of man, in the free North. He who does not perceive that a mighty wave of Anti-slavery conviction has been steadily rising for a quarter of a century in the Free States of the North, and that it was this growing conviction which, on November 6th last, secured the triumph of the Republican party, and the election of Abraham Lincoln to the Presidency, knows nothing at all of American affairs. He who, during all this time, has been able to see in American ministers and churches, little or nothing but cringing Pro-slavery subserviency, is utterly blinded: he neither knows himself, nor his country, nor his age. He is as insane as the crazy astronomer in "Rasselas," who believed that he guided the sun along the elliptic.

It is this Anti-slavery sentiment of the North, the very existence of which seems to be denied by these reverend gentlemen, or regarded as a thing of very little value, which has vindicated freedom of speech and the supremacy of law in all the Free States, which has protected not only Dr. Cheever, but hundreds o other earnest preachers of righteousness, against the violence of a Pro-slavery mob, whilst they have hurled the thunderbolts of truth upon the strongholds of Slavery. It is against this Anti-slavery sentiment of the North, that the Southern Confederacy is organized, and the present rebellious war waged. The great rebellion is not raised against the national Constitution as such, but against the dominant influence of the Anti-slavery North in the administration of the Government. The slave-power has been defeated in its purpose to govern the nation in the interest of Slavery, and is now resolved to tear it in pieces rather than permit it to be governed in the interest of freedom. It is only because the North is not such as Messrs. Cheever and Blanchard seem to represent, that the Southern slave-power makes any war on it. The present war is at the same moment a war of Slavery against Freedom, and of anarchy against constitutional government. And when a well-informed American, in a foreign land, represents the dominant sentiment of Northern ministers and churches as Pro-slavery, it requires a very great stretch of charity to hold him guiltless of slandering his brethren in Christ, and the country that gave him birth.

I am, Sir, yours, etc.,

J. M. Sturtevant,

Moderator of Council.

Andover, Mass., August 21st.

www.ingramcontent.com/pod-product-compliance
Lightning Source LLC
LaVergne TN
LVHW021417110826
845150LV00007B/1967

9781425509422